mY
GEOmYThICAL
JOURNEY

Revisiting Ancestral Bonds
- Ancestral Wounds

Anne Stewart Saunders

The Oracle Press

THE ORACLE PRESS
www.oraclepress.com.au

National Library of Australia

ISBN 1 876494 66 2

Cover painting: 'Changing Dimensions' by Laurie Love

Contents

Acknowledgements

Acknowledgements and gratitude go to the following people who opened the necessary doors. To *Mantatjara Wilson, Billy Wara, Nellie Paterson and other Pitjantjatjara Elders* who accompanied us on the journeys. *Martha and Alvin Ponga, Erina, Rihi, Ma* and all the *Ponga Family* in Wanganui and Tieke. *Wiremu Turner and Turumaranga Parnell* in Te Kuiti. *Arthur and Teresa Mahi* in Hawaii. *Hagit Ra'naan, Victor Barr, Victoria Nissan and Michael Lightweaver* in Israel. *Christine and Ross Wallis* in Ohakune for their humour and insights. *Philip Simpfendorfer and All* at Glastonbell for their support and dedication in keeping the spirit of the land alive. *Simon Peter Fuller and Pat Hall-Ingrey* for their encouragement and inspiration. *Ulli Hansen, Pippa Dickerson, Gillian Marshall and Brian Steele* for their valuable support along the way. *Lawrie Love* for the artwork *and Dorothy Pollard* for refining the text.

To Christopher and Elisabeth

"You are being asked to

Break the barriers

At the deepest of levels between the

Aboriginal and Celtic races... but

First start with the Maoris because

They are Easier."

Transmission received from the Wedge-tail Eagle, 1993.

Introduction

When I share my stories about walking the land and working with the geomancy of the earth I am frequently asked what activation, reactivation or changing the frequency of a site means. As I understand it, the body of the earth is similar to a human body. The physical is connected by streams of energy meeting at certain points on the land, like acupuncture points on the body. These may be named vortices, sacred sites or power centres. Like the human, the earth is a living consciousness which when ignored, neglected or abused can recoil into itself and remain dormant but when someone comes along saying the right thing in acknowledgement, or sounding the right note, the human, or earth, will respond and the life force will flow out. The old people also cloaked certain power sites to prevent their energies being misused when they saw trouble coming with colonisation. In New Zealand a chant in the ancient Maori language came to me from spirit, which lifted the '*tapu*', or cloak, off a site and opened it up again 'to the face of God'. At times I am given sounds and actions to change the frequency or vibration of a site. As the world and human consciousness are ever evolving and changing so is the vibration of the planet, thus many people are drawn, guided by spirit, to particular sites to work with changing the frequencies for the new world to come. A human body is used as a conduit bringing the energies of 'Heaven' and 'Earth' together.

"From out of the spirit world
They all came dancing
They danced in the wind for everlasting life
They danced the Dreaming alive."

From 'Mimi Dancers'.

Lorraine Mafi-Williams was of Thungatti/Bandjalang descent and was writing about the Seven Sisters, or Pleiadians, who co-create the Dreaming with us. At her funeral a few years ago, I felt she had written her own epitaph, as this quote expresses her own journey so profoundly. The Dreaming is real. It is the creative, regenerative force connecting the planet with universal mind, full of dance and movement, bringing new life and abundance. The Dreaming manifests strongly at sacred sites, which respond to the connective presence of humanity. For tens of thousands of years the Aboriginal people of Australia have followed the Law as given to them by the Ancestral Beings and have cared for these sites with ceremony, dancing and singing at appropriate times for the benefit of all. I came into contact with that world a decade ago when I merged with my 'totemic' ancestral travelling companion, the Eagle. The day came when I felt committed to living the highest expression of my soul's journey on earth; with that focus, an Eagle transmitted a telepathic message to me which issued from the starry realms and directed my life from then on into a journey through Aboriginal, Maori and Celtic worlds.

We are not necessarily aware of our totem companions as we travel. The Dog, the Snake, the Owl, the Lizard and the Spider have all featured strongly on my journey, connecting me with the natural world and spirit. In fact, I have been bitten by four of those – the Spider, the Snake, the Dog and the Lizard, which has left me feeling that this mode of contact is probably significant for some of us, who are not subjected to the traditional initiations of ancient cultures. These creatures will appear in our lives, to warn us of danger, protect and assist us in troubled times. When we are open enough to appreciate their important role, these totemic creatures will connect us to the unseen realms and behave as intermediaries to universal intelligence, reminding us of why we came to experience this life on earth and expanding our vision.

The stories in this book record journeys, commencing with a telepathic transmission from my Eagle totem, which changed my life remarkably, reuniting me with places from a distant past and spiritual family connections in several countries, as well as my family in the stars. The stories are shared as I remember them. I have not aimed at 'truth', technical or scientific fact, as that would confine the total experience to a particular realm, whereas the totemic and geomythical journey is multifaceted and multidimensional.

A deepening appreciation of the Aboriginal people and their extraordinarily rich connection to the land and natural environment is growing among Australians and travellers alike, as consciousness is raised and we break the barriers of our limited, heavily conditioned minds. Their connection goes far beyond beautiful landscape, plant identification and physical environmental issues. Where their ceremonies and care have been allowed to continue unimpeded by outside interference, the land is throbbing with vitality, keeping the people and the land of Australia strong, as well as enriching those who are invited into these very sacred places. The same appreciation is extended to the Maori people of New Zealand and the indigenous people of any land, whose spirit may have been trampled on but not lost. All ancient knowledge is imprinted and encoded in the land, particularly around sacred sites, lying dormant and ready to release its essence when humanity makes connection with it. Ancestral spirits wait in the silence.

CHAPTER 1

Initiatory Merging with My Totem

As a young child, playing barefoot among rocky mountains in Scotland, I stood frozen in terror and time, screaming for my parents. One foot had landed on a majestic and terrifying mountain eagle wedged in a rock crevice and while I struggled to remove my foot from its warm body, with heavy eyelids the eagle released its final breath and spirit. Adding to my trauma was the belief of a child that I had killed it. I remember most vividly the feeling I had as I looked briefly into the bird's eye. In years to come this same spirit revealed itself to me as having then entered my energy field and integrated with my etheric body to emerge as my totem, an aspect of myself. Some years later a snake that bit me in the hills of New South Wales, Australia, had a similar outcome – the Serpent being somewhat of a polarity to the Eagle in spiritual terms, as well as physical.

Some years ago, around Winter Solstice, I met a woman who had recently come to live in the remote mountainous region of New South Wales in Australia, my home for many years. She invited me to the property she was caring for, as she and other friends who work with the geomancy of the land had discovered an important vortex where several energy lines crossed at a spot far from any dwelling. It was a dramatic place set amongst rolling hills and bordered by a gushing creek. I lay down on the earth and soon became aware of the slow rhythmic drumming usually associated with Native Americans, evoking the heartbeat. At first I thought it was the pulse of the earth I could feel throbbing beneath my relaxed body. Then I 'saw' with inner vision men dancing to my right in costume and feathers, pounding the earth. They circled around me, lifted me up and placed a hide stretcher under me. I heard the words, "This is an initiation. Look into the eye of the eagle." At once I was aware of a powerful, magnificent eagle standing on my diaphragm, light grey in colour with black flecks. The eye contact transported me into the space inside the eagle's skull, which seemed to contain a vast expanse of silence, directly connected to the Creative Source. This spatial emptiness started to emit arrows of golden light that entered the Sun and a Sun beyond the Sun to Infinity. Later, when I shared this experience with my friend, she told me this confirmed something for her, as a few days previously, in meditation, she had been asked to go to that same spot with pencil and paper. She was to draw symbols, which would allow connection with other realms. Although she did not consider herself an artist, the first drawing she had received was an exquisitely executed eye of the eagle. The accompanying text revealed a date, precisely the time that had been made available for me to go to her land. I had bonded with my totem. We had become as one and my understanding of the world I lived in altered dramatically. I began to 'Walk the Land' in a conscious manner.

CHAPTER 2

First Communication
With an Eagle Messenger

In the forested region of inland New South Wales where I lived for almost two decades, wedge-tail eagles soaring high above the plateau and over the vast expanse of ancient forest, now National Parkland, are quite a common sight. We lived on the edge of an escarpment, which dropped dramatically into wilderness where dense foliage stretched out as far as the eye could see in all directions. The land was often cloaked in mist but on a clear day a band of blue on the distant horizon marked the Pacific Ocean.

Eagles started to make contact with me – circling directly above me, flying lower and lower while transmitting a strong vibrational message, which would form into clear telepathic words of passionate communication. This did not apply to all eagles; some may just be enjoying the flow of the thermals or scrutinizing the land for prey as raptors do. The spirit messengers deliberately make contact in significant and unmistakable ways, such as hovering close above one in small circles or behaving in some extraordinary way.

One of the early, most dramatic communications I received from a large, powerful eagle carried these telepathic words: "You are being asked to break the barriers at the deepest of levels between the Aboriginal and the Celtic races but first start with the Maoris because they are easier!" I was told that this had not been asked of anyone before and I would have to tread very carefully as I may lose my life if I were to put a foot wrong. This was a large black, brown and white eagle and I felt the tri-coloured feathers were meaningful. The energy of the contact had enormous strength but I was unable to conceptualise the message. From my scant knowledge of the true history of the lands in the last two hundred years, I could imagine great barriers would have been created between the races. However, I had no direct experience and besides 'at the deepest of levels' travels far beyond the last two hundred years, to the beginning of time – to the Ancestral Dreamtime. I had never been to New Zealand to meet a person of Maori descent, nor in my 20 years in Australia had I met an Aborigine, except in spirit. There were few opportunities as the Aboriginal people from the area where I lived had almost been wiped out in the genocide times of colonisation and their descendants were only in recent years slowly returning.

My meeting with the eagles could happen any time. On one occasion near home a wedge-tail frantically circled above me, and then flew up to a high ridge clothed in ancient Antarctic beech trees. The eagle circled above the trees a few times, then returned to circle tirelessly above me again and again, until I took notice. Finally, and reluctantly as the way was steep and it was an unusually hot day, I made my way up to the grove of trees. Despite being hidden from view by the trees, it was easy to follow the eagle's directions as the energy it was transmitting down to me drew me like a magnet. When I stopped, I noticed I was inside a perfect circle of trees, within this, half hidden by accumulated leaf mould, lay a circle of small rocks, the only ones I could see around me. I had fallen into a deep state of silence influenced by the eagle's connecting vibration. When I lay down on the ground, inside the rock circle and closed my eyes, I felt the presence of an elderly Aboriginal man and his wife and with my inner vision, saw their faces. They gently told me it was time for the true history of their people to be told and acknowledged so that a healing of the past could begin. They requested that I walk over to the flat rock surface nearby, right on the edge of the escarpment. Once there, waves of deep sadness overwhelmed me. The elderly couple told me that this was where they and their families had been herded like cattle and, with orders and prodding of rifle butts, had been led to the edge to drop to their death far below. Men, women, children and even babies made their final journey in total silence. They told me that this tacit agreement was to leave a spiritual message recorded in the land that 'force is pointless'. In this way the sad history of the area was shown to me unexpectedly.

Not long after this I had a meeting with some Aboriginal elders and families at a friend's place and, like many of my culture at that time, I found some of the younger members to be rather aggressive and angry, without truly understanding why. They were saying that they were ready for the truth to come out and on hearing my story this same friend took me to another sacred place on the edge named 'Darkie's Point'. (We gave it another name, 'Dark and Light Point'). A geology researcher from the local university was negotiating with these elders to write their story. Both he and the elders needed to know where the bones were located. The elders confirmed to me that it was time for the truth to be told and acknowledged. On the way we had to pass through some remote bushland and I immediately felt the past – of being chased and then hiding in the bushes, breathless, to dodge a bullet. We were talking about the need for the people to forgive and move on. I sat down quietly at the very edge of the cliff, high above the forest, when a large eagle swooped down so closely that my friend who was behind me screamed but I was already feeling the familiar vibration of telepathic transmission, as it circled closely above my head. This vibration brought to my inner vision a picture of a swirling red mass of liquid and alongside it appeared a swirling black mass of liquid with the words, "The red is our blood, the black the land. The black is our skin, the red the land. We are one. How can we forget?" The feeling was overwhelming and I understood.

As time passed, I was relaxing in front of a roaring log fire one winter's evening, engrossed in the crackling embers. As often happens in the silence, I became aware that spiritual contact was being made. I was being visited again by the elderly couple I had met in the ring of stones in the Antarctic beech forest. They said they would like me to go down to the bush below the escarpment, to where there was a meeting of the three waters into one pool, "but," they implored, "tread very gently as the bones are down there." At a time I believed was chosen for us I set out with two like-minded friends, across the undulating paddocks in a 4-wheel drive towards the edge of the escarpment. Lois, a woman the same age as myself,

Karsten a strong younger man, who took a didgeridoo with him and I, had no idea how we were going to make our descent into this dense wilderness area of the New England National Park. We would have to negotiate tremendously steep and foreboding bluffs restricting access. However, on reaching the edge, a large brown hawk came flying out of the bush straight across our path in front of the windscreen. We stopped. An eagle appeared from the other direction, flying towards the bush and disappeared into the foliage. We left the vehicle and followed his flight path through the bushes. Sure enough, there was a narrow break in the cliffs, which over the years the heavy rains had carved out. Although very steep, we could slowly make our descent. All three of us have our own stories to tell of this remarkable day.

We had set out in what was obviously a mild trance, taking no provisions, water or matches, torch, newspaper, candle, warm clothing or anything else one might require for survival in the middle of a high altitudinous winter! Time was irrelevant. Even our descent was laborious but Karsten deftly climbed down well ahead and became our trusty scout. At first I was lagging well behind both of the others, immersed in the energies of the place, when I heard the voice of the old lady say, "Stop and go up to the left. This is where the bones are. Please bless them and take their trapped spirits with you that they may be set free where the three waters meet." Just after that, energy already dwindling, I caught up with the others beside an enormous old tree whose trunk was hollowed out at the base. "Lie inside the tree and it will give you strength and courage for the next part of the journey," whispered the voice of the old man – we were not alone on this journey! My head and shoulders fitted neatly inside the trunk and once imbued with the magnificent energy the tree offered, I came out. That was when we noticed that inside the trunk, exactly where my head had rested, was a round flat grey rock with red ochre piled high upon it. As my head had just rested there and as no one ever came to this wilderness area, which was ochre free, it was one of those things that cannot be readily explained. We painted our faces with the ochre and continued our descent under the protection of the old growth forest. At length we came upon three cascades from the narrow creeks, all tumbling into one beautiful pool of crisp, clear, icy water. The three of us sat at different points around the pool, spontaneously forming a triangle. There seemed to be three of everything, including three hanging bird nests delicately attached to trees around the pool. Karsten played the didgeridoo while Lois and I sat quietly and felt the resonance growing stronger with everything around us. Progressively we became colder and colder, shivering, had severe flu-like headaches, sore throats and generally felt extremely unwell as the energies of the past caught up with us. This, we were told, was because they wanted us to understand how it felt for them – the few who miraculously escaped death and had to flee for their lives. We agreed to create a triangular column of light and gently and silently we invited any trapped spirits to use it to go home in freedom, up towards the light of their spiritual abode. Many souls left and when we got up to return home, we felt weak and tired. It was becoming bitterly cold – the only black frost of the year (if not the century) was to occur that night. Karsten went on ahead, showing us which route to take, as we now just seemed to be in a mass of dense forest. None of us had anything to indicate what time it was but it would obviously be essential to return reasonably quickly if we did not want to become engulfed in darkness and unable to find our way out. However, reasonably quickly seemed impossible.

It was a painful and exhausting journey back towards the top. We were very cold, tired and hungry and lost our way time and time again, coming up against gigantic cliff-faces defying any hope of passage and having to go around and around to find a way up to the next level. At times the way was so steep we were clinging onto tree roots to scale a sharp rock face and Karsten had to give us a helping hand many times. At one stage we just all lay down completely exhausted when one of our treasured native lyrebirds burst into song, treating us to one of its entrancing melodies. From the depths of despair, I shouted, "Oh, just shut up!" which evoked some feeble laughter and has been remembered with mirth ever since. On we struggled again, crouching on narrow ledges to keep our balance, now realising we were re-enacting an actual scene from the past. It became bitterly cold and the sun was setting somewhere, as it was getting quite dark where we were in the trees. It was not a night to sleep out as we were ill-prepared. Turning to spirit I whined, "Don't tell me you have abandoned us?" An immediate answer came back through the ethers, "Of course not," the surety of which gave me a final burst of energy and a few steps later, lo and behold, the bush opened up to reveal a grassy clearing. We were home and to greet us stood three large red kangaroos looking humorous with the backdrop of a glorious red sunset.

CHAPTER 3

Glastonbell

The eagle had drawn me into powerful, high vibrational realms. The magnetic pull of this frequency eclipsed any interest I felt for the dense material world. I found myself making a very deep commitment to follow the highest expression of my soul's journey. At home in northern New South Wales, I became aware through dreams and meditation that my connection with the eagle was giving me an overview of the planet. Like the eagle, I was flying higher and higher circling above the land where I was to be working. Automatic handwriting indicated that I would be living in the Blue Mountains. Almost instantly I received a phone call from a friend in Sydney to say she had some money and, as my house was up for sale, would I like to join her in going to the Blue Mountains to look for land for a healing centre. On the way to the Blue Mountains I met another friend, who told me about 'Glastonbell', a sacred earth sanctuary at Bell high in the Mountains. We arrived at Glastonbell around New Year to find the caretakers were leaving for the weekend and we had the place to ourselves. We went for a walk on this well cared for property consisting of 400 acres of pristine land. As so often happened at Glastonbell, some of the people connected with the place were having major personal issues. The atmosphere was unsettled to say the least and my friend decided the place was not for her but I had a meditation in the cabin set aside for that purpose. A few minutes into the meditation, a magnificent golden Being, showering golden drops around filled the entire cabin in front of me. Telepathically he introduced himself as Jove, the God of Expansion, saying, "If the place was perfect why would you be asked to come here?" I had never experienced anything quite like this before but I got the picture.

Two months later I returned to Glastonbell with my daughter and stayed until 22nd July of that year. We lived in the caretaker's house and my daughter attempted to study by correspondence. Philip, the owner and custodian of Glastonbell and three other people were living there at the time. With the overview given by the eagle came many visions of my future work. Before I came to Glastonbell, I had a vision of myself being led by the hand of another and flying through the gully at, as I later realised, Glastonbell. He was taking me close to the rocks on the side of the gully, showing me a quartzite layer and saying, "Look closely at it." As I did it began to sparkle like clear crystal. Then we flew up to the top of some rock formations where he showed me a pool of rainwater, saying, "Look at it," and as I looked it turned into pure gold liquid. Finally, we flew to the top of the sandstone formation called 'Dreaming Rock', towering high above the valley, where a semi-circle of glowing white Beings were seated. They called themselves 'The Great Beings' who had ascended. Welcoming us, they told us we would be working together at Glastonbell, bringing the sacred sites into a unified energy.

Over the next seven years I would always go to 'Dreaming Rock' before and after any journey, where I would receive useful insights into my work. This was a completely new field of experience for me. Firstly, I had to be shown what union meant within myself, the male and female aspects, which is why the young male friend, whom I had previously seen in the vision had turned up at Glastonbell. I recognised him by the energy immediately. The strong and unusual energetic connection between us, which we both felt acutely, was like that of being twin brother and sister. The association led to my having an androgynous experience whereby I 'grew' a male body, which felt most peculiar. The memory entered permanently into the cellular level but I had difficulty returning to my normal state until I was given a vibrational chant from my Pleiadian friends in spirit to change the energy back to the feminine.

The Pleiadians came in strongly to work with me now and would further awaken my memory as to where I had come from and why I had chosen to be on earth at this time. I was reminded that my spirit had once sojourned in a star in the Pleiades called Celaeno where my work was also that of bringing elements into union. My birth name is also Anne, which means union.

When travelling overseas an old Native American medicine man called me into his tipi and asked me if I wanted to know my totem from his lands. He told me I was Grey Horse Walking Between the Nations Bringing Peace. I was shown that Eagle, Hawk and Owl act as messengers from the Pleiades and other spiritual realms. At Glastonbell I was directed to sleep in the caves. Each day I would awaken with very clear knowledge of where I was to go on this powerful land, where many Beings have blended into the landscape. I began to have contact not only with the Ascended Masters (whose energy I was very familiar with) and the Pleiadians who revealed themselves to me in a particular form but also had further contact with

Aboriginal people in spirit, including the 'as below' version of the Pleiadians. These manifested as three friendly Wandjinda, who would run joyfully alongside me wherever I walked the land for the next few years. I encountered three Aboriginal men in spirit, who said they were sitting in a cave in the Kimberley region. They wanted to sit with me in a silent circle of peace for the next three months. This, they said, was to avoid bloodshed at the Australian Olympics (this was in 1993, seven years before the event!). For three months, whenever I closed my eyes to meditate, the three men would appear with the one closest to me looking deeply into my eyes and piercing my soul. We would enter into the depths of silence for some minutes.

One night I was awoken in the 'Sleeping Cave' with an enormous angelic-like eagle flying towards the cave with its giant golden and black wings outspread. It came straight into me and I fell into a deep sleep. When I awoke in the early morning and looked out of the cave I saw a scene from another realm of existence, with vividly coloured palms and flowers. I heard the word 'Paradise'. Another time I was awoken with someone shouting, "Adjustments. Political." Looking up on the cave wall I could see a map of Australia being outlined on it, followed by straight lines being drawn across and up and down. Then a laser beam of energy came in to end with a dot at a certain location. When I later looked at a map I saw that this spot marked Wolfe Creek Crater in the Tanami Desert, Northern Territory of Australia.

CHAPTER 4

Indigenous Gathering at Ulladulla

Back home in northern New South Wales, I noticed a colourful brochure in the window of the local health food shop, inviting people to participate in an Indigenous Gathering at Ulladulla, on the South Coast. With my 'instructions' in mind, the brochure aroused my interest but logistics prohibited my participation and I filed the idea away. Then I received a telephone call from Glastonbell friends, inviting me to join them on a trip to an Indigenous Gathering at Ulladulla. Someone had cancelled and there was a place in the car. They rented a cabin for me to join them if I wished.

Ulladulla proved to be a very powerful and significant journey for me. I was expecting to meet some full-blood, desert Aboriginal people from Central Australia, considering I was being asked to journey in their land to Wolfe Creek Crater and had no idea of what that might involve. Many tribes from all corners of the globe participated in this gathering. It was intense and there were quite a few skirmishes between the local Aboriginal people and the American organisers. 'White' people were no threat there. Tagged 'Visitor' as opposed to the 'VIP' pin allotted to all indigenous people, they were completely insignificant on this occasion. The 'VIPs' were served first at meals and the 'Visitors' had to stand back and wait a very long time at the back of the queue. It was a colourful and vibrant collection of people who met there. There were talks, music, art, dancing and ceremonies for days and nights. Egos were clashing for importance, emotions running high and it was also a deeply healing time, for many stories were shared and tears of empathy flowed.

I mingled with Australian Aboriginal people as well as others but without making any real personal contact whatsoever. Instead, I found myself on every possible occasion, at meals, ceremonies, talks and other activities, seated or standing in the one vacant space next to a Maori person. In retrospect, going back to my 'instructions', this made complete sense. The Maoris, I had been assured, were easier. (I was to balk at that notion many times in the following years). There were several Maori tribes present and each time my contact was made with those of a particular tribe, the *Ngati Rhurhu*, Night Owl Tribe, from the Wanganui River in the North Island of New Zealand. Each time I met the Ngati Rhurhu it was an electrical, passionate connection. There was no doubt that those in spirit had a plan for us.

Our gathering took place on a large paddock alongside the beach and ocean. At about 2 a.m. one morning when a blue moon was in the sky but partly hidden by cloud, I was with a group of people enjoying the rich, vital music of an old blind African man. Insistent words filled my head until finally I had no option but to take notice of them. I was to walk on the beach and meet someone there. I made my way over to the water's edge and walked the length of the beach as far as the eye could see. It was a most beautiful night but no one was on the beach so I dismissed that idea and turned around to return to camp. As I did so, I saw in the distance someone appear from the camp area and walk in my direction but alongside the dunes. It was impossible to distinguish what nationality or sex this person was. However, as we slowly approached each other on opposite sides of the beach an overwhelming power directed me diagonally across the beach to meet this person who was experiencing the same phenomenon much to our embarrassment but seemingly out of our control. We met in the middle of the beach, embraced without exchanging a word and stayed in that silent embrace for some time. It turned out to be a Maori man with wild, generous hair and a gentle face. We talked for some time of owls, dreams, the Pleiades, prophets, eagles, geomancy, land, the earth grid, unity and visions. Alvin and his family shared a very similar vision to mine and, referring to me as a sister, he invited me to visit their home in *Aotearoa,* the Maori name for New Zealand.

In the end some measure of peace was achieved at Ulladulla. The dancing ladies from the Centre had travelled by bus, which had broken down somewhere along the way. They arrived late one night towards the end of our stay when the air was not only cold but also electric with friction. Painted up and wearing only their black skirts, in their purity they managed to pull everyone together to 'walk together as one, shoulder to shoulder' (including 'Visitors'), which was the slogan for the meeting. Feeling the cold they all made their way through the darkness to the Sacred Fire of the Native Americans and huddled around the flames. Not a word was uttered although previously anyone who ventured inside this sacred area, which was the domain of the Storytellers, had been balled out by the USA security guards, for being 'disrespectful'. Just as later that night, the American organisers tried to allow only the perceived 'elite' to dance with the desert ladies, the dancers gently but insistently invited everyone to join them – and everyone did! For me it was the climax of the gathering and a magical thing to watch.

I still find these desert people extraordinary in their simplicity, humanity and purity. I made no verbal contact with these Aboriginal women but the contact was made nonetheless and we were to meet again at a later date. First the Maoris because they are easier!

CHAPTER 5

Aotearoa

Eagles and owls of all colours and species came more and more into my environment. They visited my garden in the small country town where I lived. Watching, listening, hovering, protecting, waiting. A large silvery grey eagle appeared at my kitchen window one morning, a type I had never seen anything like before, celestial in appearance. Owls would stand guard on my washing line outside my back door at night. The 'Ancestors' were watching and waiting.

It was time to make my initiatory journey to *Aotearoa* – very inconvenient in practical terms but one that could not be resisted. The magnetic pull was too strong, a sensation I would often experience in the years to come.

My first stop was Glastonbell in the Blue Mountains. The custodians of Glastonbell had for many years worked with the earth energies and planetary grid and maintained close contact with friends in New Zealand. It was they who provided a bridge, arranging for me to meet an elderly couple on arrival in Auckland, who then took me up to One Tree Hill, a well renowned landmark in that city.

We sat there quietly at a discreet distance from each other, when I was surprised by the sound of a woman's voice coming out of the evening mist from across the ocean. The woman who now appeared before me had been a significant presence at Ulladulla but had returned to her homeland early and I had not spoken to her. Her name was Rose. She was wearing a traditional headband woven in flax and was carrying a *Pounamu Patu*, or Greenstone weapon.

The Greenstone has been sacred to the Maori people from ancient times and was often encoded with sacred knowledge by ancestral owners or carvers. It served as a connection to the spirit world. Despite the weapon, which to me signified the female warrior of old, she was welcoming me to the land with the haunting call of the *Karanga,* which was to become so familiar to me and which hits one directly in the heart, seeming to penetrate deeply into one's soul memory. It conjures up feelings of being in the presence of many great Ancestors, Maori and Celtic, who have a shared origin. The feelings go back a long way, to the beginning. Is this where the barriers cease to exist, at the deepest of levels? This was my first introduction to the depth and strength of the Maori *wairua*, or spirit.

My kind and enthusiastic hosts took me to some of their favourite places on the land and at home gave me an egg-shaped Greenstone to hold. I went to bed and fell asleep with the stone lying on my chest, only to be woken up in the middle of the night with it vibrating violently on my body. Telepathic words entered my mind. I had no idea where I would be going after Auckland in the short time I had available away from my children and I needed clarity. I had been given the names of several Maori and '*Pakeha*', or European, people to contact. Now helpfully I was hearing from the stone the merits, demerits, purposes and consequences of visiting the various people named on my list.

From Auckland I journeyed on to Lake Taupo, where an elderly lady long associated with Glastonbell met me. She lived on a small acreage of very powerful land in Taupo, which significantly had a female area on the lower part of the block and a large male rock on the higher part. The land was open to the public and had attracted many people from all corners of the globe. Ceremonies were frequently performed there and a spiral of large rocks surrounded by a great variety of trees had been created for the use of visitors.

The weather was overcast and cool when we arrived at her place early evening. However, I immediately climbed up on the male rock where I sat facing Mount Tauhara, the sacred mountain on an island in Lake Taupo. At first I distinguished a woman's face on the side of this mountain, then the Being projected her energy towards me with such force that I lay down on the rock. From below me a strong, white root seemed to rise up into my spine with the stern words, "This land wants Maori to walk on it." It was getting dark and it started to rain. However, I felt unable to move for a while as I absorbed the words, which had come to me, as if the energy emitted from the Being of the mountain was pinning me down.

Finally, I returned to the house and asked my new friend if Maori people visited her land much. She told me that she was wondering why they did not but thought it may be because the purpose of this land was to bring in energies for the new earth. The following morning a carload of Maori people from Auckland turned up and many have since visited and no doubt continue to do so.

My friend understood the crystal realms. She had many specimens from very large quartz Earth Keepers in the garden, to hundreds of smaller ones, which she worked with in a healing way. Covered in crystals, I lay on her massage table in the turret of her house, which looked out onto Mount Tauhara. "Ask what you need to know most at this moment in time," she suggested. The question that arose in my mind was, "How do I break the barrier at the deepest of levels between the Maori and the Celtic races?" Even before the question took shape, the same Maori woman who had greeted me on One Tree Hill appeared, this time carrying a *tokotoko*, or carved walking stick. She said, "Let's start with you and I." We looked into each other's eyes and souls for some time. Eventually, the distance between us evaporated and we communed as one. Smiling, she offered me the carved *tokotoko* and, much to my surprise, I thanked her for acknowledging me but did not accept the stick: "Because," I said, "I walk without tools." Much healing seemed to take place and I was beginning to understand an aspect of the barrier.

The following day a man from the United States arrived to give my friend a large smoky quartz crystal for safekeeping, which had been smuggled out of Tibet and through China. He said he wanted to take me to a cave on the edge of Lake Taupo. On arrival, he smudged the cave with sage and left. As I lay there in the peace and silence of the cave by the water's edge, I was filled with sadness and asked, "How do I break the barrier at the deepest of levels between the Maori and Celtic races?" A songbird entered the cave, perched itself beside me and burst into jubilant song. Again my heart was opened and the cave was filled with joyfulness. This was another clue for me.

Back at the house my friend felt strongly that I was to visit the Wanganui River Maoris, which confirmed what had been transmitted to me through the Greenstone egg in Auckland. She gave me some old photographs of Matahiwi, a very special Marae on the Wanganui River, which she had been involved in helping to renovate in her younger years. This was an interesting connection as the grandmother of the family I had met at Ulladulla had taught her many of the Maori ways and crafts there and I already had the name, Matahiwi, noted in my address book. This grandmother was one who actively promoted and encouraged peace and unity among all people, while some others in the region preferred to practice the black arts and had certain uncontested strengths in that area.

Having checked the bus timetable for Wanganui, I rang the house of the Maori man whom I had met on the beach in Ulladulla the previous year. I announced myself and said that I would like to come and visit them. With the usual Maori warmth mixed with a little hesitation he said, "Yes, I can't see a problem with that." I told him that my bus would arrive around 1 p.m. that afternoon, which was a bit of a shock to him but in the circumstances I think it had to be. My Greenstone egg in Auckland had warned me that the Wanganui people would not trust me at first.

CHAPTER 6
Wanganui

As my bus pulled into the Wanganui depot, I noticed Martha, the wife of the Maori man, was there to meet me. This was to be the beginning of a long and deep friendship. I settled into the back of the car while she and her cousin sat in front. I felt their hostility acutely but was not surprised. Eventually, they explained to me that there was a lot of anti-*Pakeha* resentment about at the moment, as clashes with the Government were reaching a crescendo and they had just come from one of those meetings. The Maoris are a warrior race and do not take kindly to being talked down to. At that time, the Maoris and the *Pakeha* Government seemed to have as much appreciation of each other as two dogs going for the same bone. The bone was land and all the issues around that subject.

On arrival at the house, I discovered that the second wife of my friend was in hospital about to give birth to her first baby. I was left at home with the other children (about five of them) while the adults returned to the hospital. After some time Martha returned to the house and we talked. I told her that I had been warned that they would not trust me at first. She admitted that these had been her first thoughts when her husband had announced my intentions to visit and she was wondering what I wanted from them. However, she said her *Tupuna,* or Ancestral Guides, had warned her that I had been sent by spirit and if she did not change her attitude they would lose me. So, she said, she realised that she had to relate to me from her higher self to my higher self.

The eagles of *Aotearoa* are now extinct but the Maori people will tell you that there was once a large golden eagle that they revered as sacred. Nowadays there is an abundance of brown hawks, which the Maoris simply say are 'our Ancestors'. They are quite accustomed to these birds bringing them signs and messages from the other realms. By this time I had already noticed brown hawks doing strange things around me while following my movements closely. For instance, they would fly low alongside the bus I was travelling in, as close to the window where I was seated, as possible. When I told my Maori friends about this, it was no surprise to them at all.

At the hospital the baby was taking his time to be born and someone

Martha at lookout over Wanganui River.

came back to the house saying the mother-to-be asked if I would go up to the hospital and join the family in the birthing room. As I entered the hospital room I was greeted with a loud scream as the baby was finally ready to meet the world. Parents, the children and grandmother all had mattresses on the floor where they slept in wait. At the moment of birth the grandmother got up and said the *karakia*, an incantation or blessing for the baby before he was rushed off to a humidity crib, as his breathing was faulty, then flown with his father to a hospital in Christchurch, South Island, followed by a concerned hawk to the airport! *Kahu Rere Tete* (Hawk Flying High) was aptly named and had made his entrance onto the planet.

While the rest of the family gathered in a circle back at home, other family members were summoned and we joined in a *karakia* for *Kahu Rere Tete*, each saying a few words, including myself, as we prayed for his safe return. He and his father did return safely and today he is still larger than life, keeping those around him well entertained. Somehow the whole incident around *Kahu* bonded me deeply with this family and although we may not be in contact for months at a time, the bond is always there.

As I had no previous knowledge of the Maori, other than a totally distorted version from my British history books, it was a very welcome surprise to me to find out how deeply they were connected to the realms of spirit, especially nature and the environment. I could talk about my experiences with them quite openly and we discovered that we shared many visions. They not only seemed to consult with their elders before taking an action which may affect the whole tribe but also sat quietly and consulted the *'Tupuna'*, or 'old people', who continue to guide them and work with them from beyond the veil.

It was after such a consultative process that it was decided that I should be taken up the Wanganui River to a sacred area called Tieke. The grandfather drove me to a Maori village at the end of the old river road. Along the way, we stopped at a lookout high above the winding river and *Koro* asked me how I felt as I looked down at the river. "Do you feel like you have come home?" I did. The place felt so familiar. At the village, Pipiriki, we stopped at the house of the boatman. I was to return here many times over the years and wait for the right time to go up the river in 'Tieke Lady', the Tieke jet boat. This might happen the day I arrived or a few days later. Despite slight suspicion from the Maori people that first visit I soon felt like one of the family and all were happy and rightly proud to share with this *Pakeha* the spiritual beauty and essence of their very sacred lands, which the Department of Conservation DOC call National Park. I instantly empathised with them and the more I saw and learned, the more that feeling was to grow in strength alongside a commitment to carry out my unfolding spiritual purpose.

CHAPTER 7

Tieke Marae on the Wanganui River

The boatman was a capable, silent and endearing companion on the river. He knew every nuance of this extraordinary river's moods and one felt totally safe in the hands of an expert as one rode the rapids. The river held its dangers and over the years some have drowned as well as revelled in its unrelenting rapids. If one has the psychic sight to see spirits, they are everywhere along this river and not all are friendly. There were several men in the boat, all going to Tieke. It was a thrilling ride, that first journey, and ever after. The cliffs and lush vegetation are a beautiful accompaniment to the experience of travelling through the wilderness and up this most sacred river. The overwhelming feeling, however, comes from the Ancestors, whose watchful presence pervades this spectacular land, which was once their beloved home and which many had never left in spirit. It could be felt for the length of the journey, welcoming one home and illuminating the way. They had in fact opened the psychic doors into their realms. One was transported back a long way in time and felt very honoured without really knowing why. It felt as if one was being received with the greatest respect, either like a highly revered guest, a Goddess or an important and loved member of the family returning home.

When the jet boat pulled into the pebbled beach at Tieke, some of the younger family members rushed down the steep banks to meet us and carry the packs and provisions up to the Marae area where we would eat and sleep. Others stood at the top waiting with welcoming smiles. Once greeted, I had to wait aside to be welcomed onto the Marae in the traditional way. This meant entering through a separate gateway with the Maori people who were 'to take me onto the Marae' once we heard the haunting call of the *karanga* go up from the senior woman. This is the cue to start walking towards the benches where the men sit in front and the women behind, the visitors calling back their greeting to the hosts as they walk. At first the guests sit on the benches with some distance between them and the hosts, who stand facing the new arrivals. The most senior man acknowledges the Ancestors of that particular area and welcomes the guests to the hearth of Tieke then offers a *karakia*, or prayer. Then a truly enchanting *waiata,* or song, will be chosen – usually one associated with the environment. The women sing this in perfect harmony, after which the guests may sing to them in return, if they wish, although it is a hard act to follow if one is not too musically inclined. Everyone is seated and talks by the men continue back and forth as the guests prepare to offer a *koha*.

These customs go back to ancient tribal times when intertribal relationships were tenuous to say the least and had to be treated with caution. Things have eased up a little these days but it reminds one of the Campbells and Macdonalds of Scotland. A *koha* customary at a Marae is not quite the same as a donation but was usually given as food or some practical thing in return for the hospitality the guest would be receiving. These days sometimes money is appropriate. It is placed on the grassy area in the middle of the Marae between the two parties and is received by a member of the host tribe, who picks it up and walking backwards returns to his group. The protocol continues, giving thanks for the gift then everyone may relax and come forward in a line for a handshake, hongi, hug or kiss from each host family member as they stand in line for the greeting. This greeting is very warm and inviting and one is immediately welcomed into the family. The hosts and guests have met with the blessing of the ancestors from both sides. A cup of tea is offered which removes the intense spiritual energy of the welcoming process, the *tapu*, and all returns to normality – that is, you get to help with peeling the potatoes for dinner and washing up.

Layers of steep forested bluffs and hills on three sides shelter Tieke, the river borders the fourth. The Ancestor of these middle reaches of the river is Tamahaki and the families, who now look after the area, are the descendents of this ancestor. A lengthy and expensive court procedure to recover their land was just in its infant stages when I first visited. A few months previously, the family had decided to go back onto Tieke and set up camp there as they had learned the Government was proposing a large international sale and tourist development along the river. They were considered to be 'protestors' and posses of police and Government officials would arrive in vessels to threaten arrest and imprisonment.

As far as the families were concerned they had just come back home and maintain that position today. I will not go too deeply into the politics of the situation here, but they had well established documentation to show that their land had been taken in the first half of the twentieth century to 'build a railway', a project which never eventuated. The older people were born, raised and, those who had passed over were buried on that land so there was never any doubt in their minds regarding the rightful ownership of the land. The Maori people had suffered a similar fate at the hands of the English colonisers as the Aboriginal people in Australia. They were poisoned, diseased, shot and drowned in large numbers. When returning to their land the elders kept the fire in the hearth at Tieke constantly burning. These people regarded themselves as the Keepers of the Sacred Fire and adhered to spiritual principals as much as possible, while many others were yet again tempted by offers of large sums of money from the Government, to compromise eventually on a tourist deal, which finally may be the only option. The court decision in their favour may never be handed down and the meetings with DOC may continue but the integrity of the land, its sacredness and its people remain in tact.

The young children wanted to take me down and show me the pebbled beach by the river's edge, singing their *waiata* all the way. Playing with the pebbles I felt the familiar vibration of the eagle and looked up to see a hawk circling wildly above some *pongas,* or tree ferns on the bank high above me. His energy and mine became one and I fell into the familiar trancelike state. I took the children back up the track and returned to where I had noticed the hawk, climbing for the first time up these steep, muddy hills of the New Zealand bush, holding onto convenient roots to lever myself up. When I reached the cluster of pongas, I noticed one large, round stone, similar to the ones that marked the ancient graves of ancestors in the *urupas,* which I sat on and waited. Shortly, I heard the words, "Your Celtic Ancestors were here and we thank you for returning at this crucial time. Please bring your children back here sometime."

Being ignorant of the history, and it seemed to be back well before anything that had been described in my old books, I was quite surprised to hear that. Beyond my grandparents, being Scottish on the maternal and Irish on the paternal side, I had no knowledge of my Celtic ancestry or even any interest in it, like most of my generation. However, there has since been a revival of interest in these ancient roots and it was to become clear to me that the Scottish, Irish and Maori people have suffered many of the same fates at the hands of the English – only in Scotland it had happened several centuries earlier.

When I returned to the Marae I found that another boat had arrived with more family members, whose support was so vital to the morale in these early days. People, not always young, had left their comfortable homes and lifestyles to protect this sacred land for their children and future generations. It was a dedicated task to remain in this isolation for long periods at a time, depending on the boat to deliver essential provisions.

Being a DOC stop on the Wanganui River, where thousands of tourists pass in canoes each year, Tieke Marae is open to tourists to spend the night camping and join the family for dinner. Sometimes this involves cooking for up to a hundred people at short notice but this was never any problem to these tribal people. Often the tourists, including intrepid New Zealanders, were experiencing a Maori Marae for the first time and were truly fascinated by what they learned there. The warmth, the welcome and the humour were all very different from the media coverage about the 'protestors'. An opportunity was never missed to put them right about the true political situation either, of course, which had been opportunely distorted by the press, to the extent that many *Pakeha* tourists thought boulders might be hurled down the slopes to greet them.

Among the family members to arrive was one whom I had met and talked to at Ulladulla. He had been talking there to a group of people around the Native Americans' Sacred Fire about the Pleiades and the Maori spiritual worldview. I briefly shared some of my Pleiadian and Eagle connections with him at Ulladulla and he also suggested I visit the family in *Aotearoa*. This man was a leader and had a certain power within the tribe at the time. The people depended quite strongly on his many talents and knowledge of the old Maori ways and language. The Maori people are very eloquent when they speak their language or talk about the heritage. This man was one of these talented orators who speak holding a carved *tokotoko*, a walking stick which may be imbued with ancient knowledge from past ancestors or the carver himself and which may serve as a link to channel an ancestor's words. Here at Tieke I exchanged a few words with this man and was very surprised by the words that came from me. They came from another source, which later revealed itself to be Pleiadian. This was to occur many times when speaking on the Marae and sharing in a circle with the Maori friends, an indication of the presence of the Ancestors on these powerful sites. I told him that the tribe would only be allowed the ongoing custodianship of the land if they stood in their full integrity. Having recourse to anger and angry outbursts lost energy and diminished that integrity. The Maori historically are a

Canoes on the Wanganui River.

renowned warrior race and the tendency was to be moved to extreme anger with officials who would have them evicted from their land. My words, coming from a *Pakeha* woman to a male Maori warrior, were totally unacceptable and inappropriate under normal conditions. However, the Pleiadian energy that brought forth the words rendered them undeniable. I had no idea at the time why I was saying this but it was met with acceptance by this man, whom I shall call Rangi for reasons of privacy, with whom I realised I was to have a very strong connection in this spiritual journey involving breaking the barriers.

I went to sit quietly in the forest waiting for the jet boat to make its return journey to Pipiriki until I heard the others calling me. I quickly collected my pack and ran down the bank towards the boat, where the other passengers were already installed. My warrior friend was standing by the boat to my right as I descended and as I was about to say goodbye to him and get in the boat, a hunter came from my left carrying two black and white goats by their hind legs. Both had been decapitated and they drew me in. The words that came were, "There have been two sacrifices in the past." I turned to Rangi on the right and found myself saying, "But there is no sacrifice this time?" "No", he replied. I said goodbye and climbed into the jet boat, which departed with the blessing of a *waiata* sung by the women up on the banks.

What on earth was I talking about? Tears began to flow freely as the boat sped off and visions entered my mind of two occasions long ago when Rangi and I had been involved in a sacrifice when the earth shattered and for which we felt responsible. They were only fleeting impressions. One involved a great rock wall where tall slim sacred men stood on guard around 20,000 years ago. Inside the walls young women were taught the art of love. The earth shattered and the place was destroyed. This rock happens to be across the water from the cave at Lake Taupo where the American had taken me, the male and female polarities. The second impression was arriving in an ancient Celtic vessel and meeting the darker races there but in unfortunate circumstances. Once again, I took a big risk considering my position vis-à-vis this warrior and the whole tribe but somehow I had to express the strong impressions and emotions I felt. Before leaving Wellington airport headed for Sydney, I wrote a letter to Rangi describing in detail the impressions I had received and why I said what I said to him. The following year, when we next met, he told me that he had really understood my letter.

CHAPTER 8

Uluru – The Red Centre

On my return to Australia I headed for Glastonbell in the Blue Mountains. My first port of call was Dreaming Rock. Certain sites in Glastonbell seem to be able to link a person into anywhere on the globe and I made a very strong connection with Wolfe Creek Crater. So strong, in fact, that I could see it as the pupil of an eye and as I did so my left eye began to flicker and became quite painful. It was to remain like this until I had completed my task at the crater.

From Glastonbell I returned home where my didgeridoo-playing friend and I sat to tune into the purpose of my next trip. An eagle had once transmitted a message to me with the words, "Look through the eye of the eagle." At first I thought it meant that I look into the eye, as I had done previously. However, my attention was drawn inside the skull of the eagle looking out of its eye and I felt the deep silence the eagle experiences as it is directly connected to Source. Sitting beside my friend I now saw myself as a golden eagle flying over desert. As I looked down I saw a tall, slim, old Aboriginal man lying on the sand. His feet were bandaged and he could not walk. He had white hair and beard and was wearing a red headband. When he saw me he raised a delicate black arm and beckoned to me to come down. "Hurry up! Hurry up!" he was calling. As I flew down my body changed into that of a human but still had the head of a bird.

I was to learn in time that the Eagle, Hawk, Horus, Toth, Owl, Thunderbird and Phoenix are all interchangeable in the worlds of spirit and was to have connection with all at various times.

I rubbed the old man's feet and he put a scroll into my beak saying, "Take it to the key people quickly." I then flew further north and landed, again turning into half-human, half-bird. Another Aboriginal man was waiting for me. He took the scroll, read it and imprinted the words in gold glyphs into my chest: 'Knowledge turns to wisdom in the heart' and he showed me three colours. The blue of the sky, the head the white races; the red of the sand, the desert, the lower chakras, survival, the Aboriginal race; the green of the land, the heart, the Maori race. "Quickly," he said, "Take it to the key people you are to work with."

From this inner vision I realised it was time to go to Wolfe Creek Crater and that I would be connecting with some Aboriginal people. I consulted my map and worked out the route to Halls Creek via Alice Springs on the Greyhound bus. Quite a journey but it was necessary that I travel overland. A friend knew someone in Alice Springs and asked if I may stay with him to break my journey. He agreed and it was only when I realised I had to go to Kata Tjuta as well that I rang him to ask for advice on how to get there. His suggestions about renting a 4-wheel drive and staying in motels in the Yulara tourist resort did not sound right, so I asked him if he knew why I was coming. He said, "No. I only know your name is Anne." I told him I was just coming to sit on the land, guided by spirit and his mood changed. He said that two Aboriginal medicine women had asked him who was coming. He said he only knew my name was Anne and they told him that I was to come and stay with them at Mutitjulu, the community at Uluru.

When I stepped onto the Greyhound bus with my backpack and sleeping bag that first time, I had no idea what was in store, having never ventured further than the southern and eastern coastal areas of Australia. I still had not met in person in any real way, an Aboriginal Australian. I had made my initial contact with the 'key' Maori people I was to work with and had been totally accepted into the family. Now the Aboriginal contact was to be made. This back and forth situation between Australia and New Zealand carried on in stages for seven years and continues today but on another level.

In a state of complete ignorance, trust and surrender, I arrived one sunny afternoon at the Outback Pioneer Motel in Yulara, where the Greyhound left me. I rang the Mutitjulu Aboriginal Community number the women had given for me. The phone rang out many times but no answer. I wandered into the motel and asked if I could order a taxi to take me out to Mutitjulu (in 1994 there were still taxis there). Then I discovered I did not have the obligatory permit to enter Aboriginal land and would also have to buy a ticket to enter the National Park on the way. No taxi driver would risk taking me without a permit, as the laws were too stringent at the time. After a cup of coffee and more surrender, as it was getting late in the day, I rang again with the same result. Once again I went into the motel just in time to catch a young taxi driver who had just dropped off a client. After repeating my request to him, he shook his head and said it was too risky for him to take me to Mutitjulu but he would take me to the Ranger's office in the National Park and ask him how to proceed. I had the names of the two medicine women I was to visit so something could perhaps be worked out there. We arrived at the Ranger's office about three minutes after the Ranger had gone home for the night. I remained completely still in my seat, my mind silent while spirit worked it out. My driver reluctantly said that he would take me but if we were caught he/I or probably both of us could be fined $10,000 and spend the night in the lockup. I said I felt comfortable with that possibility and would take full responsibility, as I was certain the Elders and Law people at Mutitjulu were above and beyond bits of white man's paper when it came to the crunch. (I have since discovered that they are – when it comes to the crunch). Arriving at Mutitjulu Administration Office my driver said, "I sure hope your contacts are good because I am just going to do a U-turn and get out of here." He dropped me off, turned and fled. I thought this to be rather strange but no doubt he had his reasons.

When I later told the traditional owners of the place, there was much laughter but then they were quite angry at the ridiculousness of the situation. Then again, I could have been inventing my story and names to the driver in order to infiltrate without a permit and snoop around for whatever reason.

I asked a group of teenagers who were gathered outside the office where I could find Mantatjara. They told me she was in this office building at a meeting with the Elders. Someone brought her out and we looked at each other. Mantatjara is a huge lady, dark and blind in one eye. I was small, white and thin and one eye was almost closed due to pain. I said, "I am Anne, may I stay here or not?" She told me to wait a minute bringing me a chair and said she would go in and speak to the Elders, disappearing back into the office. A few minutes later she re-emerged, saying that I could stay for one night and we walked to her house where she showed me 'my' room, which she had set up very thoughtfully for me. She left me there while she returned to the meeting, producing some photograph albums to look through. I had the company in the house of her uncle and auntie who also lived there but did not speak English. The old man had white hair and beard, wore a red headband and was lying down with sore feet. Mantatjara had asked me if I would massage his feet with some Maori bush medicine she had. He was the man I had seen in my vision who was telling me to hurry up. No words were exchanged, as I do not think Billy Wara speaks much English but none were needed. I am his sister in

Aboriginal skin language. I opened the photograph album and looked at the photographs of Mantatjara's overseas cultural trips and there she was in several photographs with my Maori friends in *Aotearoa*. It was beginning to look like there might be some kind of structure to this unlikely plan.

In the evening Mantatjara came home joined by several other ladies, all sporting T-shirts bearing the words 'Night Patrol'. These women had taken it upon themselves to go out at night and intervene when they saw any of the young men drinking too much, as alcohol was prohibited on the property and caused untold problems when that rule was overlooked. I was left alone in the house. Shortly after I went to bed a young woman burst into my room saying her husband was in hot pursuit. We looked out the window to see her car blazing and beyond her car she told me her parents lay bashed by the drunken men. I told the young woman to hide under my bed and I sat quietly reading. When three men staggered into my room, guns blazing so to speak, they seemed to pale at the sight of a white woman in bed there and retreated at great speed.

Mantatjara returned with friends and some teenagers. The women slept on mattresses on the floor of the main room in the house as was their preference and chatted and joked well into the night with my friend translating for me.

The following morning my friend told me that she wanted to take me to the Rock (Uluru). In fact, her house was right at the base of Ayers Rock and it felt as if we were already there. She asked me if I wanted to take my camera or whether I wanted to climb it. I only wanted to feel its energy and that certainly did blast me as the Landcruiser entered its energy field. Tears were streaming from my eyes and seeing this Mantatjara took my arm saying we would go to ceremonies at a women's sacred area for three days.

I stayed a few nights at Mutitjulu then one morning we set off along the Docker River Road in the old Landcruiser, packed with ladies eating KFC, swags, digging sticks, paint, food and sticks for clapping and dancing. When we stopped I saw that we were just behind Kata Tjuta, the other place I was to go to but had not imagined it would be like this. Some older women came in from tribes in the different directions and met for the ceremonies as they had done for thousands of years. Physically it was almost unbearable for me there as my eye was pounding with pain. The eye was connecting very strongly now with the energy of Wolfe Creek

Mantatjara with the author near Ernabella.

Crater, which looks exactly like the pupil of an eye and in fact is such to other realms. It had been aching since I left Sydney and I had spent most of the Greyhound ride with a chamomile teabag pressed against it to ease the pressure. It was also excruciatingly hot by day and at night we slept together in swags under the full moon after the ceremonies. Somehow the energy was not conducive to sleep for me. It was a truly magnificent and powerful sight watching my friend dance with her stick beneath the full moon, the silhouette of Kata Tjuta towering on the horizon. The other women and I were sitting clapping sticks and chanting. Small fires were lit. I felt lucky to be living in Australia, a land where such powerful ceremonies are held to enrich the country and our spirits. I am not at liberty to talk about 'the women's business' nor would I be able to because no words were exchanged between us, as to what they were doing. My part was to be with the energy, which took me down deep into the earth and made me feel even more nauseous than I already was because of the eye condition.

Well after dark we would get into bed with our swags lined up alongside each other, a small fire burning between them until morning to keep the chill of the September night at bay. A medicine woman was involved in healing a very sick old lady next to me who had been beaten by her husband in a drinking session the night before. She smelt strongly of alcohol and as the medicine woman whispered healing sounds into her ear, while stroking her gin and blood-matted hair with butter, I became acutely aware of the unconditional sisterly love that the people had for each other.

I was moving in and out of realms constantly by this stage and by day I would ask my friend if I could walk to the dried up riverbed which was lined with beautiful red river gums affording better shade than the saltbush. This women's sacred stream formed one of the curved boundaries of the area where these ceremonies were performed. In a daze I staggered across the desert to the river and sat there for a while trying to adjust to the reality of the circumstances in which I found myself. Was it real? It was very hot and dry during the daylight hours and I wished for water flowing in the river instead of the red-hot sand. I felt I had to get away from everyone for my sanity and after I gained enough composure, I would return to camp. Nothing was said.

The next time I needed a break, I asked my friend again if I could walk to the river. She told me I could but asked me to choose another track – because the unseen track I had taken was one the women had walked on to get to this sacred area for thousands of years to participate in ceremonies. I took another way, rested by the river for a while and then returned to camp. Again, nothing was said.

The third time I asked to walk to the river, my friend once more asked me to go a different way because I had walked on another track used by the women for thousands of years. On my third and last walk I sat by the river for a long time because I felt no longer in this world and my eye was excruciatingly painful. Added to that I was nauseous with the feeling of entering a very heavy vibration deep inside the earth. Eventually I staggered back and just wanted to return to the world I had so willingly walked away from. On the return journey I became aware of masses of wriggling, translucent pink snakes crossing the path back and forth in front of me. They blended into the red sandy desert floor, revealed only by their agitated movement. My mind had slowed down to such an extent that I can remember thinking to myself that I should be careful not to stand on any of them, as I made my way through the seething masses, which was just about impossible but did not concern me too much. Back at camp my friend asked me if I had seen any wild camels. Family groups of marauding wild camels in these desert lands have been known to attack people. I said that I had only seen hundreds of snakes. "Snakes?" said my friend in apparent astonishment. However, the following year, when talking with her in New Zealand I asked her what these snakes were that I had seen. Her answer was clear. She told me I had been on the snake women's track and that it was their snake totem acknowledging my eagle totem. The things these people say so casually never cease to amaze me. I had not mentioned anything much at all about myself or what my purpose was, let alone declaring an eagle totem.

A very interesting thing I found about that first encounter with the Aboriginal women was that my identity and purpose seemed to be irrelevant and what needed to be known seemed to be felt by the people. I found them to be refreshingly intuitive and relished the fact that I did not have to explain myself in terms that people were meant to be able to understand. When any of the elderly women asked my friend why I was there she just put her hand to her heart and then translated for me that the women said they were happy I had come.

I felt very weak and tired and my eye was intensely painful when we drove back to Mutitjulu. At the clinic the community nurse gave me drops for my eye but, as I suspected, the eye did not improve. I still had a long journey ahead to Wolfe Creek Crater and I hoped my eye would heal once in contact with the spirit of this crater. Quite frequently, when working with geomancy, my body would take on and hold the blocked energy of the place I would be working with. My friend and I drove with some other community members to Alice Springs, where a physician friend also provided eye drops. The drops did not help.

CHAPTER 9
Wolfe Creek Crater

Physically and mentally my time with the women at Mutitjulu and the ceremonies had been exhausting. I was aware that I was being tested and also learning a lot as it was necessary for me to be strong and clear about what I was doing before I entered the energy field of the crater to carry out what was being asked of me. The eagle back home had warned me that I had to tread very carefully or I may not survive and I think I was being put through an initiation, not so much by the women as by the spirit Beings who had arranged this journey for me. Later, I received a telephone call from a Maori woman from the Wanganui River, who said she had a dream at that time. In the dream I was walking up the middle of the Wanganui River towards a row of Aboriginal Ancestors who were watching me intently. The energy was intense and felt dangerous. Then from behind me a row of Maori Ancestors appeared and after greeting the Aboriginal elders in the traditional way they told them that they had opened their doors to me. The Aboriginal elders then started to walk towards me until we met and embraced. I was constantly aware of the spiritual presence which had merged with me and was moving me forward on my journey and this made me quite at ease with myself and confident about my work despite constantly walking straight into the great unknown.

At Glastonbell, an old Aboriginal man in spirit had told me that they would send two warriors with me to the crater for protection in the form of two wattlebirds. These two wattlebirds flew close to me and stayed with me at Glastonbell. They were easily distinguishable from other wattlebirds by their energy and feeling of connection as they followed me across the land. When I returned home further north the first thing that greeted me was the sound of two wattlebirds and they were never to be far away.

At this time, however, Mantatjara seemed to feel the task was beyond me especially with my physical condition. When I said I was going out to book a ticket on the Greyhound bus she asked me if it was for home. When I told her it was for Halls Creek and thence to Wolfe Creek Crater, she indicated that she thought I was deranged. I left her there at Alice Springs and many hours later was removing the chamomile teabag from my eye

and parting with the bus at Halls Creek terminal.

Halls Creek, at that time of the year anyway, seemed like a one dog town. I had very limited funds which made my situation even more unlikely than it already was but I approached the tour office there to enquire about the 4-wheel drive tours to Wolfe Creek Crater about 500 kilometres at least down the Tanami Track in the Tanami Desert. This seemed to be the only way to actually get there but as there were no other tourists for the tour, it was definitely not viable just to take me. They suggested the joy flights which covered the Bungle Bungles, a few other sites and Wolfe Creek Crater. That seemed totally inappropriate since my usual energy work involved actually sitting on the earth not flying over it. After some time, however, and having checked out all other possibilities and hit a blank wall, I asked about the flight. Again this was not possible because there were no other tourists and I only had enough money to cover one person – they needed a minimum of five.

With that I returned to the tourist park and bought a cold drink thinking that I was in a singularly interesting position, having travelled thousands of kilometres in a bus to get here only to find I was unable to reach my destination. I sat quietly with a still mind, surrendering yet again to the situation I found myself in. Those of us who work with spirit are accustomed to reaching a point where we say, "OK! Good one, Spirit. Over to you now." I had reached that point when suddenly a dapper young man, sporting a neat brown suit and haircut, dark glasses and an unusual little smile, approached me.

In fact, for a long time after that I thought about how unusual he was generally and wondered from out of what reality he had appeared. His words were, "I will take you where you want to go." His appearance was similar to the young taxi driver who had first taken me to Mutitjulu, when I had also reached the point of delivering the whole matter up to spirit. I told him that I wanted to go to Wolfe Creek Crater. Still smiling he asked me to follow him. A Japanese tourist then appeared out of nowhere and unable to speak English managed to indicate that he wanted to come too. Goodness knows what he thought of the joyflight. The next part is hazy and otherworldly. We walked to a car in a dreamlike way and drove to a small plane, seeing no one on the way. I also realised I had not seen this pilot in the office where I had just been given a very definite no to my request but realised that some newly qualified pilots are keen to log up the necessary flying hours to meet their qualifications. It did not really matter as my purpose was to get to the crater and this was now happening against all odds.

Once seated in the tiny plane, the Japanese man squeezed into the back and I sat in front beside the smiling pilot. No words were spoken. We flew straight to the crater and started circling it in a clockwise direction. For some reason, I counted how many times we went around and think it was 14 but am not quite sure. I do know that when he changed direction and circled in an anti-clockwise direction he made the same number of rounds, which seemed to create, or open, a vortex. My whole body meanwhile was shuddering with the energy working through me, and, as is usual when involved with this work, I was in a dazed state compounded by the eye. I was thankful my companions were not the reactionary types. The crater looked exactly like the pupil of an eye from above and it was huge, apparently the second largest crater in the world at 900 metres across with walls 55 metres high. I heard that the Aboriginal people of Western Australia say two great Rainbow Snakes made it and when I took a photograph from the window of the plane a circular rainbow ball appeared on the floor of the crater. Finally, the plane flew straight across the middle of the crater before leaving and as it did so an enormous wedge-tail eagle hit the windscreen in front of the pilot, blood and feathers splattering everywhere. The pilot did not react at all which astounded me and this valiant, feathered messenger came with a warning to me that the energies, which were now being transmitted through me, were so strong that I would be blinded temporarily but not to worry as it would soon pass. Through me an access point to the inner earth for the Pleiadian energy was being opened, for whatever reason was not for me to know. My thoughts are that these two young men, the taxi driver and the pilot were sent from spirit if they were not in fact from spirit themselves but I could be wrong. Back at the tourist place, I could in fact no longer see and the pain was tremendous. The blindness did pass after a couple of hours and I stayed in Hall's Creek overnight before catching the Greyhound bus back to comparative normality the following day.

Several days and nights later I arrived back home on the east coast of New South Wales, my left eye still flickering and far from fully recovered much to my dismay. In this state I was shopping and socialising at our local country markets when a friend spotted me and said she could see a dark cloud over the left side of my head and covering my eye. When I briefly related my tale about the crater, she suggested I come up to her house and she would do some healing on it. Once back at my friend's house, I lay back and relaxed into a very deep state to go into the silence that is required for deep healing. My friend, who is a veteran healer asked the appropriate questions and from my unconscious mind ancient memories were revealed.

Where I was lying I became aware of three Pleiadian spirit friends to my left and three Wandjinda people to my right. These were the six companions in spirit who had been travelling with me since I started walking the land. The Wandjinda would always be running along happily by my side as my footsteps became light and fast and energetically they were the inner earth version of the Pleiadian energy. They were reminding me of the reason I had chosen to come to earth at this time and they worked with my body to remove the heaviness and pain around the left eye. I then became aware of myself as one of the Ancestral Beings from another realm whom the Aborigines speak about in their stories of the creation times. I materialised on earth at the location of Wolfe Creek Crater and had come to work with the dark-skinned people of earth there. I tried very hard to fulfil my mission but found the heavy vibration of earth too difficult to maintain in my lighter materialised body. The feeling was reminiscent of that which I had recently experienced with the old ladies at the ceremonies near Mutitjulu.

I felt very nauseous, so I left sorrowfully saying, "I will come back." That 'I will come back' had left a thought-form that became 'embodied' by a spiritual Aboriginal guardian of the crater. My eye condition was persistent and I could still feel an irritation there until my friend massaged my feet. Then I understood that the guardian who held the thought-form was a part of me that I had left behind long ago. As I felt this energy approach and enter my being we were reunited and the eye instantly returned to its normal condition. I was learning many things that had been out of my range and probably seemed a bit preposterous beforehand. I had indeed come back to Wolfe Creek Crater, which was no mean feat and my eye was now restored to health.

CHAPTER 10

Pakaitore

It was natural to me now to fall into deep meditative states on a daily basis for lengthy periods, sometimes up to five hours. I was continually receiving guidance, wisdom and support from the spirit worlds and was deeply committed to following my spiritual path. Besides my children, nothing else was of interest or relevance to me. I seemed to have had such a full life encompassing every experience I had wished and was now free to pursue my journey from a much deeper and richer level of understanding.

This commitment is very different from anything else, in that one immediately has the sense of its totality. One literally is in a state of being where everything evaporates and only emptiness remains, in order to be the receptive vessel that is required for this journey. Once commenced, it was not long before my partner went, my house went, my money went, interest in employment or hobbies went, fundamental beliefs went and my two children had to meld into this new form our lives were taking. Never for one minute have I doubted the direction my life has taken since then, although it has been a great challenge at times in the physical, mental and emotional sense. Finances have been ridiculous on paper most of the time but this has never interfered with my needs or my journey and I am asked to travel a great deal.

Glastonbell has always been a point of inspiration and creativity for me. The owner, Philip, always had helpful insights about my journey to share. The Beings who have chosen to reside in the land there have always been able to give me relevant information about the next step of my journey and, as is now a well-documented fact, the earth like the body, has connective energetic pathways, linking the whole. Glastonbell was strongly linked to the various places I travelled to and it was at Glastonbell that I learned about geomancy and to walk the land in a conscious way, open to receiving the subtle energies she offers up. This well cared for land taught me to open up to and work with earth energies. On the first Sunday of each month for years people would gather in Linking Cave on the property and in meditation would link with each place on the grid we were consciously connected to, keeping these links strong. In the evening, whoever wished would climb up on Sunset Rock and enjoy the peace of the sun setting behind the hills on the other side of the gully. Sometimes the wedge-tail eagle would be flying above and messages from beyond the veil would be transmitted.

One day I had been sitting quietly on this rock enduring an unusual headache that had plagued me throughout the day. As I left, it occurred to me to ask spirit to take this pain from me. I jumped down from the rock and a small wagtail flew around and around my head. I stood still thinking the bird was trying to get my hair to make a nest. It was hard not to laugh as its beak gently touched my forehead but did not pull my hair. When it flew off into the bushes, my headache had completely cleared and I gratefully acknowledged the part this little healer had played.

Towering above the Vale at Glastonbell lay two giant sandstone rocks. Here, Dreaming Man would often communicate with visitors to his Dreaming Rock and Sacred Rock. Perhaps it was this being who clarified the next part of my journey for me for it was here I received a message to take Mantatjara over to New Zealand and to return to Tieke, the Marae on the Wanganui River.

This new mission sounded fairly clear and straightforward. However, the logistics were somewhat different. I was most surprised when I rang up the Mutitjulu community number in the Centre of Australia, to have Mantatjara quickly on the other end of the line and even more astounded when she answered in the affirmative about coming to Aotearoa, although I shouldn't have been.

We met at Sydney Airport and went to the house of a friend in Maroubra where we were to stay the night. This was a pleasant time and Mantatjara spent the rest of the day on the garage floor painting one of her dot masterpieces.

However, a problem emerged as her handbag was empty, meaning that she had no money at all, passport or papers with her. I only had her flight ticket for the following day plus one, which a friend had kindly paid for. So the following morning we turned up at the passport office with Mantatjara assuring me the Pitjantatjara Women's Council had faxed her birth details, etc. to the office and we only had to pick up her passport. Several customers in the passport office were having a fit because they were refused a passport due to lacking one of the many documents they were required to bring and Mantatjara had none. It did not look good. A series of people were consulted about whether any documents had been received for Mantatjara. Nothing. The Women's Council, as well as the administration office at Mutitjulu were contacted but denied all knowledge of any papers to be faxed. We sat it out, knowing that we were to fly the following day, and leaving the problem firmly in the officers' and spirit's court as there was nothing more we, or should I say I, could do. Mantatjara was pretending not to speak English and I had the anti-discrimination laws in mind, considering desert people were often born under the stars and may well not have birth certificates. Some hours later we ended up in the manager's office. She was a young and efficient Asian lady who got the picture fairly quickly. She produced a Statutory Declaration form and asked me to sign it to say that I knew this was indeed Mantatjara and state how long I had known her (I had spent about a week with her, which raised eyebrows but nothing else). Armed with passport we returned happily to Maroubra on a Sydney bus.

On the journey she told me she wanted to take me into a cave in a rock in the desert to give me strength for the work I had to do with the Maoris. I did get there eventually.

The flight was pleasant and uneventful and we were welcomed at Wellington Airport by Martha, Alvin and Erina and driven to their home in Wanganui. We did not stay there for long, however, as the Maori people were staging a major protest at 'Matoa Gardens', or Pakaitore, according to tribal history. Matoa Gardens was a public park in the town centre, adjacent to the Council Buildings with only the road and a boatshed separating it from the Wanganui River. Historically, it was a place where the tribes would meet to exchange *kai,* or food and other products and the time had come when the people of the land wanted to reclaim this important but controversial site. The usual Marae complex of buildings had been quickly erected with makeshift materials to serve the purpose. The sleeping house, the eating house and the meeting area were all there in wood, plastic and canvas. Representatives of tribes from all over Aotearoa had travelled to Pakaitore in support of this important protest, some making the journey by canoe symbolically picking up people at the different stops as a show of unification.

Frustration with Government had come to the point where the protest was bordering on a demand for sovereignty, although not all agreed with this aspect. The Ponga family were giving their support in the areas of security, preparation of meals and the many other ways the Maori people contribute to a large gathering of the people. Music and entertainment were always a special contribution from this very talented family and this helped to keep the spirits up.

This was not the only event to greet us on this trip. Wanganui had its strongest earthquake in fifty-odd years the day we arrived and the Ponga's roof had been damaged. Erina was awaiting the birth of a sister for *Kahu Rere Tete* and this time had arranged to have the baby born at home. Bahia had a natural birth on a mattress on the sitting-room floor where we all slept, as is the custom with the Maori people when they have guests. Mantatjara cut the cord of the Pakaitore baby and we were all present to bless her along with the rest of the family. Mantatjara and I were soon to be ushered to our mattresses on the floor of the *wharenui,* or sleeping house at Pakaitore where we spent most of the following week.

This week was probably one of the most intense I have ever experienced. Mantatjara again felt that I needed protection. We were, after all, in the midst of many Maori tribes whose relationships with Pakeha were not always the best and anti-Pakeha sentiment was running high. We stood out in the crowd being two conspicuous representatives from Australia, one large and black, the other small and white. Mantatjara went through a protection ritual with me from the safety of our Marae beds at the back of the sleeping house. Red hair ropes were tied around my head and upper arm, the latter one being joined to a rope on her arm. As she offered up a prayer to the Ancestors in her language, the wisp of smoke rising up from a stone she gave me to hold in my cupped hands, joined with the Ancestors to ask for their protection – at least this is what I gathered.

In working with Mantatjara few words are ever spoken between us and I have never felt prompted to pry too deeply. By the same token, Mantatjara has never pried too deeply into my work and the beauty of the relationship is that we have always accepted each other's work with the understanding that it is multidimensional and when we come together we are instruments of our Higher Purpose. Mantatjara is a Law and Medicine woman, or *Ngankere*, who works with the energies in ways to which she is accustomed.

In hindsight, that protection was probably critical, as the time would soon come when I was to need all the help I could get.

Although I had bonded deeply with a particular tribe, the *Ngati Rhurhu*, it took quite a concerted effort to remain immune from the general anti-Pakeha blasts of energy one encountered at this gathering.

Police surrounded the park, with ongoing threats of arrest and forced evacuation. There was also support from Pakeha alongside this police guard; a group of Pakeha peacekeepers kept vigil as such gatherings could become quite violent and another group of Pakeha supporters could be seen on a tower in the distance holding hands in a circle of support for peace. At one stage a Maori healer took Mantatjara aside inviting her to sleep in their family tent and not 'with that white woman'. This was one of the several awkward situations Mantatjara found herself in over there. With difficulty and not wanting to offend, she told the healer that she had to sleep where I was as we were travelling together. A tragic event, which shook the gathering at its foundations, was the drowning of a baby in the park fountain, which happened very quickly despite the crowds, and was seen as a sacrifice by some but not a good omen. It did look at times as if the protest was on shaky ground. One night police invaded the camp, saying that there had been a bomb threat, which they had to take seriously and investigate. Whether it was a hoax or not was never clarified but no bomb was found. Not taking any risks, Mantatjara asked a group of us to stand in a circle while she again used a platted hair rope and lit it to send the smoke up to the Ancestors to call in their protection and I also suspect to send a bit of evil to the bomber.

I enjoyed being with the Maori people, who were a lot of fun even in adversity. As each tribe arrived they were welcomed onto the Marae in the traditional way. Intertribal protocol was considered important and was never neglected.

We met one other lady there of Australian Aboriginal descent. Lucy had married and lived in New Zealand for many years and was delighted to meet Mantatjara. She was distressed because she had not seen her sisters in Australia for 30 years and could not find them. They were from the 'stolen generation' and had been adopted out to different families. When she gave me their names I knew of them and where I could probably find them on the east coast, as one was a well-known filmmaker and teacher, Lorraine Mafi-Williams. This was the start of a long association with these sisters when I returned to live on the east coast of Australia. They were overwhelmed to hear news of their sister and where she could be contacted.

The Maori people have the greatest respect for the Aborigines, who, they say, are the oldest people on earth. They felt fascinated and very privileged to have the presence of Mantatjara with them and ever after asked me all sorts of questions about her well-being. Mantatjara, herself, was deeply saddened to see how many of the Maori youth had resorted to alcohol, drugs and suicide like her own people due to the loss of land and culture, as she understands it.

The Maori tribes have been working hard for many years to reclaim their land and rights and have achieved a great deal towards that, especially in the last year or so after years of frustrating disempowerment. Tieke and Pakaitore were part of this movement.

To escape the intensity of the situation Mantatjara and I would go and sit on the riverbank and enjoy the peace of the fast-flowing river. This river is very sacred to the Wanganui Maoris and is regarded as an Ancestor. It is a body of water that is full of vitality and many times I was lead to consult with the Ancestors, who would communicate with me from its depths, as if the water was speaking to me as it rushed past.

One such day Mantatjara, an elderly Maori grandmother with some young children and I went to sit on the riverbank. The children helped to carry Mantatjara's paints, brushes and canvas, as she wanted to paint a gift for the Marae at Pakaitore. We sat there quietly while the children played on a muddy bank that had been excavated by council workers. One of the young boys came running over me, clasping in his hand an object he had found in the mud. When we cleaned it in the river, we saw that it was a well-worn bone carving of two birds, one male, and the other female blending into each other with an intricate design. It started to vibrate in my hand and the words transmitted to me were that it was time for the Eagle to meet the Serpent and that I had to go to a cave by the waterfall at Tieke. It was the privilege of another to take me there as an Ancestor was buried in that cave who was calling the other to work with him. That other was Rangi who at the time was one of the self-appointed custodians of Tieke and had a major influence in its inception. I was informed that he was representing the serpent energy from the planet Sirius and I was representing the eagle energy from the Pleiadian star system and these systems were now starting to come into alignment. This esoteric message did not require to be understood by me, only the overview. I felt myself fall into the usual trancelike state as I absorbed this message but did not convey it to the other until two days later.

That morning I awoke early, being asked by spirit to go down to the river. Again the Ancestor communicated with me. He said I should first ask permission from Rangi's partner before I approached Rangi about working with him. The opportunity came to me that night when the partner came over to talk to Mantatjara and I as we lay on our mattresses. Her response was, "Yes, of course you can. You didn't need to ask me." That proved to be untrue but I had carried out what was asked of me. Although Rangi would never have admitted it, we were locked into each other by spiritual connection and magnetically drawn to each other's vibration both in the early days at the indigenous conference at Ulladulla and now here at Pakaitore. This was not really an acceptable situation for a Maori man steeped in his culture, whereas I was well used to working spiritually with both men and women and had little idea that we would be drawn into some tribal conflict around it.

Although the atmosphere was intense at Pakaitore and Rangi was working with the security, he had approached me several times to share impressions of the situation but mainly to share with me facets of Maori spirituality, which are known only to the few who have been trained at one of the Maori Schools of Learning. Rangi was a great orator who held Maori spiritual knowledge, which he shared eloquently with those who were interested. It was difficult for me to follow much of this let alone remember it, as to me it was quite complex, hearing only aspects of a total system. In addition, I was acutely aware that there was an uneasy, completely polarised energy between us, which explained the Eagle and Serpent analogy. It was at this meeting that he told me he understood the letter I had sent from Wellington Airport after my first journey up the Wanganui River.

CHAPTER 11

Huruharama (Jerusalem)

At Pakaitore, Rangi acknowledged and could relate to what was asked of him through me. This request, coming from a white woman to a Maori warrior, was very irregular, particularly in the explosive circumstances we found ourselves in, playing a part in the reoccupation of their tribal lands, which was doomed to failure. However, as so often happens when spirit comes in strongly and the energy is of a very high vibration, it could not be denied. We arranged to meet some time later at Pipiriki, where the boat left to take the families up to Tieke, and all seemed surprisingly uncomplicated so far.

Martha and I left Wanganui for the river road by car. I had received an invitation from a friend who lived high in the hills above Jerusalem or *Huruharama.* Waiwai lived very close to her Ancestors and was interested in the old ways of spirit. She lived with her family, including Brett who was the man I had seen carrying the headless goats on my first visit to Tieke, on her ancestral land, which looked down over the Wanganui River and the hamlet of Jerusalem. Jerusalem is famous throughout New Zealand for a poet named James Baxter who lived there amongst the Maori people in the sixties and championed their cause amongst other topics of concern at the time. When I arrived, we ate large quantities of raw chestnuts and shared our feelings and experiences about the river, which was the main topic of interest at the time. Waiwai's next request was that I accompany her to the *urupa,* or mound, which was the gravesite of her Ancestors. She had her ideas about where she wanted to take me during my three-day stay but wanted to consult with her Ancestors for confirmation. The old people had other ideas about where I was to go and were clear about it. Waiwai was to take me to the House of Learning in the hamlet, then to the Marae of her family and thirdly to the grave of James Baxter.

At the House of Learning, after climbing through a window to get in, I sat quietly facing the photographs of the ancestors of this *wharekura,* the traditional House of Learning where aspirants would spend seven years learning the Maori arts of the Tohunga. The Tohunga was the priest or medicine person who generally held the higher knowledge necessary for the health and well-being of the tribe. At first, one photograph, amongst the many placed on the back wall, stood out and seemed to come to life. It was of a woman in traditional dress but wrapped in a flag. Somehow a healing seemed to take place between this woman in the picture and myself. Later Waiwai told me that the flag was that of the Battle of Matoa (an Island in the river at Jerusalem) where many were killed in the old days. This had been a bitter battle as some of the tribes had joined with the British troops to fight and kill their own people who stood firm on their land. Such a division goes on today unfortunately. The *Pakeha* name for Pakaitore was Matoa Gardens. Later, another woman who had seen me at the *wharekura* felt overwhelmed by my message, as she was a direct descendant of the woman in the picture and said her family house in *Huruharama* had just burned to the ground as her people were trying to reclaim Matoa Gardens. When the energy between the photograph and myself abated and the silence of the hall returned I closed my eyes and became aware of a warrior in spirit placing a *korowai*, or woven cloak, around my shoulders and thanked me for returning. I removed the cloak, thanking him for his acknowledgement, but told him that I walked without tools, meaning protection in this case, just as I had said when the carved *tokotoko* was presented to me by the lady at One Tree Hill.

My understanding of this came when recalling a lone and silent retreat I had undertaken before setting out on this long spiritual path. While sitting in meditation some very severe pain had entered my chest cavity, followed by a warm golden glow of healing light. I heard the words, "From now on your only protection is the Light." Some days later as I lay on a blanket on the veranda my spine seized up in agony. This gave way to the warmth of a golden rod flowing up my spine accompanied by the words, "From now on your only support will be the Light." How true both these pronouncements were for the years that followed. So in spirit and in the physical I handed back sacred rods, cloaks, greenstones, bones, hair ropes and anything else the tribal people had grown accustomed to use for protection against a plethora of ill doers in body or spirit. All tribal people, whether Aboriginal or Maori felt responsible and concerned for my welfare when I told them of my journey, seeing that I was totally unaware of their land and ways. Waiwai gave me an ancient piece of *pounamu* from her family's collection to carry with me when I walked on their land – for protection.

Our next stop was Waiwai's family Marae. We both sat quietly inside for a while. After a short meditation and acknowledging the Ancestors, we left with my friend exiting ahead of me. I saw a spirit leave the building behind her and jump on her back. She said it was her father who had passed over and we spent some time healing that relationship and releasing the spirit of the father.

The third stop was at the grave of James Baxter. It was he, in spirit, who urgently wanted to communicate a message through me to Waiwai. He was passionate in his desire to tell the people that although in principal he agreed to the making of the film, he wanted to be sure that his true message would be the thrust of it and not sensationalist commercialism. Waiwai told me later that a documentary was to be filmed in Jerusalem about the life of James Baxter and the message seemed to be alerting her to give her time to ensuring the authenticity of the reporting.

As I prepared to leave Huruharama a pure white arch of light, a white rainbow, appeared in the sky and we took a photograph. Brett and Waiwai had prepared a beautiful outdoor bath for me the previous night under the moon and stars. A fire was lit under the bath, which had been filled to the brim with water and *kawakawa* aromatic leaves. The *kawakawa* tree grows abundantly throughout New Zealand and makes an astringent medicinal tea, which is now very popular beyond its native shores. It is an old favourite of the Maori people. It was easy for spirit to connect with me in these circumstances and I was told that I had to leave the following day and would meet Rangi at the Marae meeting at Pipiriki, another hamlet further up the river where I was also to meet Mickey and the jet boat, 'Tieke Lady' to go up the river. I would also give Mickey money to bring Mantatjara and my daughter, Elisabeth, up the river the following week to meet me.

Unfortunately, our first stop was the veranda in *Huruharama* of a friend of Brett and Waiwai, where everyone, besides myself who only drank copious amounts of water on these journeys, was drinking beer. As time is of the essence with these spiritual meetings and as the cans lined up against the wall I could see my driver, Waiwai, was progressively getting into a less and less ideal state to ensure I would reach my destination. I reminded her that time was running out for me and would she mind taking me to Pipiriki while she still could. She told me she could drive that river road with her eyes closed, which may well have been true but I did not fancy risking it in the circumstances. Fortunately, Brett stepped in before Waiwai got into full warrior mode and drove me to the Marae at Pipiriki where I met Rangi. Although I did not go out of my way to attend these tribal meetings, when I did it was always useful for me to have some knowledge of how things were going politically alongside the spiritual.

Rangi and some of the other male custodians of the middle reaches of the area were wearing white headbands and were obviously on a mission. Rangi told me he could not come with me, as he was obliged to do some *mahi*. *Mahi*, meaning work, is also used for spiritual/political work or tribal obligation. I was very surprised and disappointed that Rangi could not come – not in a personal sense but because of the fact that the request had come directly from spirit and the time factor seemed important. My work in 'breaking the barriers' with the Maoris first because they were easier, was extremely difficult and intense at times because of energies which I was holding and which were working through me, as well as the political and racial tensions abounding at that time. Any hitch like this brought it close to breaking point. However, I continued on up the river, which always transported one into other mystical worlds.

My appreciation of the Maori and Aboriginal people and their Ancestors extended through the very special feeling of abundant love, which emanates from the land they have cared for over many thousands of years, through the constant connection between the physical and spiritual realms. Whatever other aspects cause doubt, their experience of connecting deeply with this land is undeniable.

CHAPTER 12

Tieke and Rabbit Flats

It was always a pleasure to reconnect with Larry and Maree Ponga, the senior resident couple, and descendants of the ancestor, Tamahaki, who had committed to looking after the very sacred land of Tieke on the banks of the river. There were traces of a former *pa,* or village there and standing stones marked the graves of Ancestors on the mound of the *urupa.* I visited Larry and Ma many, many times at Tieke, brought many friends to meet them, and spent time at their other home in Raetihi. In their controversial role, they had resolved to stick to spiritual ways even in great adversity at times and always fully supported my work. Without them and others there, I could not have carried out the work which spirit was asking of me. So although I was a person who walked the land, connected with the land and worked with the spirit of the land, I could only do so by going through the designated Keepers of that land. In this way barriers could slowly be broken and sometimes erected which was always frustrating. I learned to live in the way of non-reaction, the way of surrendering to spirit. The senior Pongas always accepted my peculiar behaviour and ways, often with a sense of humour. Larry epitomised the quick-witted humour the Maori people have when observing people and events. They will regurgitate such events again and again in storytelling and the humour never loses its edge. It certainly helped me lighten up.

Larry and Ma followed a Government program, whereby they took in young members of their tribe who did not fare well in Court to Tieke to learn about their culture, to be looked after and to abstain from drugs and alcohol. To heal addiction withdrawal, pain or anger, the young people would go and sit on the riverbank, which always brought some peace to troubled hearts. I saw many of these young people transform over the years, others have died before reaching their twenties, while others returned to their old life on the streets and were not able to rise above past troubles. They too were fun and so interested in anything to do with healing or spirit. They would confide in me about the violent, appalling situations they had experienced in such a short life because I was an outsider. Their stories were hard to believe yet the young people impressed me with their openness and loving nature despite the apparent harshness of their lives. One young boy walked with me to the highest peak above Tieke to tell me his story. It took several hours to reveal it in short sentences. Then silence before he said, "it gets worse." When it got to the very worst he could not speak it but wrote it in the dirt with a stick.

I returned to my tent one night to find two extra mattresses in there. They belonged to two girls in their early twenties. One was wearing a band of brightly coloured threads around her wrist, which she said she had taken off my backpack and replaced with a self-coloured black one. Then she asked me if she could read me a poem she had written, which was one of the most poignant poems I have ever heard. She told me she had written it a year ago for her dead sister who was beaten to death by her boyfriend before he crashed his car and died himself. This was the anniversary of her sister's death and she had replaced the black thread band she had worn around her wrist since that traumatic day a year ago with my coloured one.

Awaiting the arrival of Mantatjara and my daughter, Elisabeth, I was being drawn daily to a point on the land where spirit would communicate with me. Numerous hawks would come close then fly to a high area, a peak above the forest, indicating where I had to go. It looked very high up and without the guidance of someone who knew the way it would be nearly impossible to reach. Once again an archetypal energy of unification was to be anchored there. When the energies of several power sites were drawn together and anchored into one spot that power would be used to change the frequency for the new earth. When neither Mantatjara nor Elisabeth turned up I sent a message to the Ponga family in Wanganui that I had paid and arranged for them to come up in the boat from Pipiriki with Mickey. I received a reply from them to say that Mantatjara had been taken to the home of the Maori woman who did not want her to sleep with 'that white woman' and Elisabeth had had flu but they would get her to Pipiriki. It was good to see Elisabeth. The company of so many young people at Tieke ensured she enjoyed herself and the request of the Ancestors on my first visit to Tieke, to bring my children there, was being fulfilled.

Larry and Ma told me the area I was to go to was Rabbit Flats, farmland above the 'Watchtower' for Tieke. In the old days they would watch from this elevated platform for canoes coming down the river towards Tieke, or going up pulled by poles digging into holes made in the banks. A hawk would also fly up ahead with a warning. The senior couple accepted the fact when I told them three blue beings, announcing themselves as Pleiadians, were working with and through me. They wanted a particular energy anchored into the spot they were sending me to, which they would then be able to work with for their part in transmuting the energies for a new earth.

I never went into the reasoning too deeply with those things but simply followed my guidance in a trancelike state because I had made that deep commitment to service of spirit, healing and the earth changes. Two guides were arranged to take me there, along with a young boy and my daughter and we started our steep ascent through the dank and mystical New Zealand forest. This way was exceptionally steep and often one was startled to find oneself perched on a very narrow muddy ledge etched out by the wild goats or pigs that roamed these forests. We had several rest stops along the way and when I sat with closed eyes I would see many spirit Beings, always blue in colour. As I was seeing blue dolphin spirits swimming past me, my daughter pointed out shells embedded in the muddy cliff, which must have been there for thousands of years and held many secrets of an ancient ocean world. No doubt these dolphins had returned in spirit to this special place to welcome us.

Finally, a clearing was reached and we stepped onto a grassy plateau unseen from below at Tieke. This land belonged to a *Pakeha* farmer and the Maori people, who were still seen as a threat by many such people, had been warned that they could get shot at if they trespassed. Not worrying too much about that we sat down under a tree and unpacked the sandwiches and drinks we had brought for lunch.

Before I had time to eat mine my body was drawn to a spot to our right where some tall trees had been allowed to remain standing. By the time I sat down with my back against one of the trees I had fallen into a very deep meditative state and soon my body was vibrating violently for a few minutes, similar to receiving an electrical shock, as the powerful energies were being transmitted through me.

I am always in a very deep peaceful state after these experiences are over and when I opened my eyes I saw that two wild paradise ducks were at my feet. They are always in pairs making the dual male and female sound as they fly and they express the concept of union to me perfectly. It is very sad to see a lone one if its mate has died as they are then quite lost. They flew off and as I followed their flight path, a large blue shape appeared, looking like the classic spacecraft, and out of it climbed the three blue friends from the realm of the Pleiades, smiling, happy, congratulating and celebrating. Perhaps this was to confirm that one was not alone in this mission. Another confirmation which has come time and time again with this earth work is the appearance of a rainbow, no matter what the weather, a few droplets of rain and often an eagle or hawk. At other times, a sudden change in the weather would occur, such as strong winds or storms with much thunder and lightening. This is how spirit speaks to many who walk the earth and work with geomancy and the spirit of the land. It feels very rewarding after the strenuous effort it often takes to accomplish what has been asked of one, especially when going in more or less blind. I am not a particularly physically strong person but I think it is fair to say we were all pretty well exhausted by the time we returned to base. The men had carried long sticks with them, which we sometimes had to hold onto to jump from one steep ledge to another and the descent was no easier than the ascent.

Dinner was ready for us in the large canvas-covered dining room. At one end of this was a huge open fireplace and chimney. Two oil-drums filled with water, each with a tap were permanently in place above the coals and a side fire could be used for oven cooking in the coals or toast. Besides this fire, that was constantly kept alight, there was a large gas range for cooking and everyone helped with the preparation of food, cooking and washing up. The system worked extremely well and the ambience was always warm and cheerful in the dining room against all odds at times. Before eating, Larry would stand up in front of the fireplace, facing the people gathered in the dining room and bless the food and after dinner would again stand and offer up a *karakia*, a prayer of thanks to the Ancestors before introducing himself to any visitors, translating his prayer and welcoming everyone to the hearth of Tieke. The *karakia* was followed by an introduction and sharing of feelings, experiences or whatever else both hosts and guests felt they would like to offer. As each person took their turn around the dining room the others would listen with great interest, feeling the presence of the Ancestors who had gathered here for many long years.

After the introductions on this night, and weary though exhilarated by our arduous journey, we joined the group of guitar players and fire makers by candlelight around the sweat lodge. The sweat lodge was just the place to unwind with the beautiful, gentle music of the guitars and singers outside under the stars and moon. This work has its spectacular rewards.

The following day a group of women, guided by Tania, arrived in several *wakas*, or canoes. A blessing is always asked for the journey before the canoe takes to the water and a fern leaf placed at the helm. Sometimes a conch shell will be blown; a karanga or a special *waiata* will be sung to the guests as their canoes retreat into the distance, just as it has always been. Tania, a well-experienced river guide, was taking a group of women down the river and teaching them about working with the earth mother.

Once again, after dinner, the fire and several candles were lit outside the sweat lodge. As a group gathered around, Tania and the women entered the lodge and filled the small space to its capacity. After a short time one of the women who suffered from asthma had to leave and Tania beckoned to me to come and join them. It was a privilege to enjoy the sweat lodge for two nights in a row with so many wanting a turn but it seemed, and turned out to be, appropriate. The others were sharing their experiences on the river as I sat in silence not wishing to intrude on their group experience. Then Tania started to teach them about a blue energy that would appear at Tieke, so I shared my story with them. Tania was delighted to hear it because, she told me, Grandmother Kitty with some other Native American companions had recently come to Tieke. They had asked to be taken to the same place where I had been earlier that day to connect with an energy there, which they had brought down and stamped into the earth, as is their custom, on the spot where the sweat lodge was to be built. I never knew or confirmed whether some of the stories I heard in Aotearoa were true and in the state I was in I was never sure from which realm I was hearing the words but there was always a beautiful weave to the process.

The following day Elisabeth and I took the jet boat back to Pipiriki where we had arranged for Martha to meet us. She arrived with Mantatjara and the atmosphere was leaden. Whatever barriers were to be broken had reared their ugly head in no uncertain terms in my absence and both Martha and Mantatjara were weighing heavily with it. Further down the river road we stopped at Matahiwi, a very peaceful Marae, and went for a walk to the river. I allowed the other two women to walk ahead of me and sit close together by the water's edge while I waited under a tree higher up the bank. After a short time, Martha approached me indicating that Mantatjara had a problem with me, or my attitude. Although I knew it was Martha who was experiencing a problem, largely because of some tribal affiliations, it was clear to me that many discussions about white people had been taking place in my absence. Due to the hurt of the people around the Pakaitore and other land issues this was not surprising at the time. Somehow these feelings had to arise and be expressed before any real healing between us could take place. Once home I heard that certain family members had reprimanded Mantatjara and Martha for mixing with a white woman and confusion had arisen. When Martha left us to go into the kitchen, Mantatjara said she had a bad headache (a familiar occurrence) and asked me to do some healing on it. While massaging her head and sending her healing through my hands I suggested to her that if she had a problem with white people she start with me, as that is what I was there for. She said she had no problem with me because we had walked together for thousands of years but the others were talking... and her headache disappeared. The Maori healer, who had wanted Mantatjara to sleep in her tent at Pakaitore, had taken Mantatjara to rest at her house, which was why she had been unable to come up the river to Tieke. I was sorry she had missed a visit to this very special place but she did have a good rest with her friend. It was during this time that Rangi probably received strict instructions from some areas not to work with me. I always received full support from others who had the appreciation if not the full understanding of what was happening and why I was sent. Their orators could recite their *whakapapa*, or genealogy, back to the stars, including the Pleiades, which I was shown in an ancient document regarding the art of carving, so what I was saying was not unusual to these people. However, acceptance proved difficult as the extended tribe included an element of radical thinkers at this time.

Stone ancestor from Wanganui River.

CHAPTER 13

The Gift of the Grandmothers' Stone

Mantatjara, Elisabeth and I flew back to Sydney where Elisabeth joined the father figure who had raised her and to whom she was very close. Mantatjara and I returned to Karla's house in Maroubra for the night. Karla is a young artist with great talent. She wanted to come with us to Glastonbell in the Blue Mountains and the following day we caught the train to Bell. We had to exchange trains at Katoomba and in usual Aboriginal style we sat down on the platform and got into conversation. We missed our connection and had to take a taxi. I was the only one with any money and when we asked the taxi driver how much the fare would be to Glastonbell, he said it would be $50, which was exactly what I had in my wallet. There was a good gathering at Glastonbell on this occasion, which included several people from overseas as well as Australia and it was enjoyable to sit around the campfire and catch up with so many people with similar interests. Mantatjara enjoyed a lot of attention and received a few massages. She liked the land there very much and the land enjoyed having her. The following day Peter Fuller from England was conducting a ceremony with a group of people in one of the caves at Glastonbell while Mantatjara, Karla and I sat on a rock above them with Mantatjara singing.

Back at the house Mantatjara reached into her bag and brought out a very precious object. It was a curved, shell-like stone, in the shape of a fossilised lizard. It seemed ancient and it was really hard to imagine what it could be. She put it carefully into my hand saying it had belonged to her great, great, great, great, great grandmother, who was a medicine woman and had walked the land. She said I was to have it because I was doing that now. This made a powerful impression upon me. I had no idea that I was to have such a strong connection with the Aboriginal Ancestors. In spirit the Ancestors are certainly with us. They have guided my pathway this last decade. When I held the stone quietly, it came to me that it held all women's knowledge from the beginning of time. There were faces and bodies of women in the stone. I saw a dinosaur type of creature come out of the ocean, which on land changed into a lizard. In lizard form it was crawling along the sand, along a songline, or energy pathway, to a waterhole. As it bent its head to drink from the small but deep pool of water a blue Mayan face, shaped exactly like a stone I had found on the Wanganui River, emerged to guide it down into the water. Together they travelled underground to re-emerge at the Wanganui River, teaching me about ancient connections and timelines, which I would be working with later on. I always carried that stone in my hand when I walked the land during the following years until one day, at Uluru in the year 2000, it broke in half in my hand. Physically this would almost have been impossible and I was slightly alarmed that something may have gone wrong. However, when I told this to Mantatjara, although her first reaction was also shock, she quickly remembered something and said, "Yes. The year 2000. It's the end of the old world." This seemed sad in a way and a great loss. I have witnessed some great treasures disappearing, although this is without doubt how things are meant to be.

It was time for Mantatjara and I to part company and she headed back to Alice Springs. The Maori women from Wanganui had arranged with her to come over to attend the Women's Sacred Ceremonies in Western Australia some months later. I had offered to arrange this and organise their visas, etc., but it was taken out of my hands by the Maori healer and her daughter who had claimed Mantatjara's company in Wanganui.

CHAPTER 14
The Foothills of the Kimberleys

After my usual sojourn at Glastonbell it had become clear to me through spiritual communication with an eagle and Beings on this sacred land that my next journey would take me up north again, to Halls Creek and beyond. A friend and I set off as usual in a Greyhound bus for the Kimberley region where I had hoped to contact Lisa, an Aboriginal lady I had previously met at Halls Creek. She had told me where to find her which took us to the area I was later to connect with. When we arrived we found she had flown to a remote community to help a relative and instead we spent time with members of her extended family. I told them where I wanted to go, which was a high ridge on one side of the road. The river, and behind that another ridge of equal height, formed the boundary on the other side of the road. I was told the area I wanted to go to was the men's area and a very sacred cave with significant rock art was up there. I suspected this to be the cave where I had previously been in contact with the three male elders, who years before had asked me to sit in silence with them for three months. A woman said she would take us there but whether because of this or not, she was severely beaten in the night. The following morning the men were there to give their blessing to the journey.

My friend and I made the ascent alone. Walking on top of the ridge I knew for sure that I had walked there before as a Pleiadian. It seems strange when one is not in that energy but at the time it is very real and ancient memories come flooding back. These memories, however brief, help one to understand the stories the traditional people tell of the creation times. This was a long red, rocky ridge and it felt powerful to walk along it looking down on the vast beauty of the landscape below. We came upon a circle of stones and found ourselves involved in movements, which were to bring about a joining of the male and female aspects of the land in that area. The energy of the two ridges was connected in union. We then sat down and fell into the deep silence, which such places evoke. Straight away my inner vision conjured up a long very black, very shiny snake. Then, one by one, seven pure white spots appeared along its back and again my mind was being flooded with Pleiadian memories.

This was to be a wonderful trip into the primal experience of the Eagle

Nellie Paterson and the author at Amata.

meeting the Serpent, which would evolve into the Thunderbird meeting the Eel and lastly the Phoenix meeting the Whale, the energies always rising higher and delving deeper. We were in the company of salt-water crocodiles and eagles at Margaret River and constantly aware of their energies communicating with us as we slept under the stars in our swags. Sometimes an eagle would perch on a branch above us. We spent quite some time in the hot pools at Mataranka where a pair of large water snakes swam with us in the natural hot stream, while the eagles soared overhead.

Finally, we returned to Alice Springs where we thought it best that I journey onwards to Mutitjulu alone. It was always necessary for me to travel alone in the early days because of the precariousness of the relationships with the tribal people. I was, after all, turning up expecting to be allowed to tamper with spiritual energies on their most sacred land. Somehow, if one went in alone, the vulnerability demonstrated a certain level of trust and the necessary courage to follow one's pathway. I had to prepare and initiate myself into this position quite radically before being up to the task of carrying the purpose out successfully and this is acknowledged when one walks alone.

I was told at the Mutitjulu administration office that Mantatjara was in hospital in Alice Springs having tests. My presence here among the white people did not seem to be entirely welcome for reasons best known to themselves. I was expecting the Maori women to be arriving shortly as the ceremonies were due in two days time but was told that they were not coming and that the ceremonies were sacred and only for Aboriginal women. I have since ascertained that this is not the case. I was detecting a certain possessiveness, which I was to see more as a disempowering energy than a protective one and others were to confirm that. The level of control the administrators had over the indigenous people made quite an impression but, as with everything, things have moved on in this ever-changing world. I did manage to make contact with Mantatjara by telephone and she told me to go and stay with Nellie Paterson overnight, then come back to Alice Springs. When I found Nellie she was sitting quietly outside in the sand getting ready to light the fire for the evening meal. She showed me to a room in the house behind her, which I could share with her granddaughter. I spread my sleeping bag on the bed and went outside to join Nellie as the sun was setting. We did not speak much but I asked her if the reason the Maori people were not coming over for the ceremonies was because it was exclusively for Aboriginal women. She laughed and was adamant that the ceremonies were for all women to share and that it was up to her anyway as she was the 'boss'. I later was told that their visas and arrangements had been sabotaged by the daughter of the Maori healer in conjunction with administration in Alice Springs – the same people who seemingly had almost prevented Mantatjara from having a passport to come to New Zealand with me. Whether true or not I found the whole business quite sinister at the time but things have inevitably moved on and attitudes have possibly improved with more understanding and insight.

As the sun disappeared behind Uluru, Nellie lit the campfire and put the billy on to boil water for a strong cup of black tea with white sugar. A woman came and sat next to me. She had brought one of her paintings to show me. She told me it was a story about the Seven Sisters (the Pleiades) and upon her canvas was a shiny black snake with seven white dots. Then another came with her painting to reveal the same thing, and another, and another until a circle of seven women was complete, each bearing a canvas with a painted black snake with seven white dots. Each told me a story about the Seven Sisters. Finally, there was silence and I tentatively asked them if they knew that Beings from this realm had guided me to them. The reply came in the form of a drawing of a map on the desert floor with a thin stick. Nellie's daughter told me of a special land they had, where one day they would all live. It had special healing water and a special rock with gold flecks in it. She said I would come there some day too. The name, Umutja, was somehow transmitted to me and it stayed in my memory for several years before it was eventually time to travel there. I was always waiting for the time to come when Mantatjara would take me to Umutja.

The following morning I managed to get a lift into Yulara where I caught the first bus available to Alice Springs from the Outback Pioneer Hotel terminal. After contacting Lois, I went to visit Mantatjara in hospital. She looked very well and was ready to leave. Before departing on this particular journey with Mantatjara I had communicated with spirit indicating that, while dedicated to my spiritual goals, I would prefer my journey to be a bit easier. I asked, "How can I stop the testing?" as I had felt every inch of the way I was being watched and 'tested' by the key people I was guided to work with. While initially, I could see the necessity of it from their perspective, I felt it was no longer necessary. The reply was clear when it came "Mantatjara has acknowledged you by giving you the grandmothers' stone. Now you must acknowledge her by giving her a crystal skull." I agreed but wherever does one find such a thing? Not surprisingly, a friend had turned up the following day with a quartz crystal skull that she had found in the banks of a dry riverbed nearby. She handed it to me saying she had received a message from spirit that it was to go to Mantatjara. It had been a power tool used by the men in the past, not always for good purposes, and they were now willing to hand it over to the women. I now handed this to Mantatjara in Alice Springs Hospital and she said she would ask the men about it. She later told me she was a little afraid of it because its eyes flashed red at night.

We picked up Lois and went to the Women's Council buildings where Mantatjara wanted to use one of the Pitjantjatjara Toyota Landcruisers to return to Mutitjulu and to take us on a trip into the desert. Her request was not met with approval and while Lois and I waited in the reception area for close to an hour, Mantatjara argued in the office with the white woman who was in charge of the vehicles. She emerged fuming saying that she had a car. This turned out to be a rented vehicle, which she had paid for by demanding an advance on her salary. Mantatjara had been one of the main movers and shakers behind the formation of the Aboriginal Women's Councils and did not enjoy now being denied a vehicle although she was still on the payroll. I heard later that she had returned and smashed up a few Toyotas there with a 4x2, which would not surprise me. After our trip to the desert with Mantatjara and some of the old people, whom it was always a great pleasure to be with, Lois and I returned to Glastonbell on the Greyhound.

CHAPTER 15
The Eagle meets the Serpent

The short stay at Glastonbell was very potent with a feeling of urgency to return to Wanganui. I booked my flight to Wellington where Alvin and Martha picked me up as usual. The women had been disappointed about not being able to come to the desert to join Mantatjara at the ceremonies as they had been so inspired by meeting Mantatjara earlier on that year and wanted to learn more about her people. Everyone wanted news of Mantatjara as her presence at Pakaitore had been strongly felt and appreciated.

My mission was to locate Rangi as quickly as possible and go up to the cave at Tieke. I could not do this work alone as I had no idea where the cave was, which was why I had been told that it was another's privilege to take me there. Rangi came round to the house when I arrived and obviously was in no mood to co-operate. I had placed him in a very awkward position with this request from spirit. I could feel the urgency of spirit working through me and did not want to fail in my attempt to have him understand the situation but he was a difficult subject to attempt anything with.

There is a saying that the Maori man moves slowly. When white man is telling him something, he moves even slower and when it is a white woman he does not move at all. I can confirm that saying. Timing is of the essence with this earth energy work. When spirit starts to communicate strongly, the feeling cannot be ignored. One is magnetically pulled to the land where spirit is calling and now this feeling was intense.

With members of the Ponga family I drove up the river road one night and made a last ditch effort to talk to Rangi, who was at Matahiwi. After insulting me as much as he could, he resolutely refused to work with me and we left. The family who had taken me to talk with him did not feel good about their involvement at this stage, neither did I. In any case I felt compelled to go up the river and a few days later arrived at the boatman's house in Pipiriki to take the jet boat up to Tieke. I don't know which of us was the more taken aback when arriving at the boat. The only other person going up to Tieke was Rangi. This looked promising in a way, other than his attitude, which had not changed. As luck would have it the boat broke down halfway up the river and in the silence of the wilderness around us we had to get used to the proximity of each other's company for a while. It was impossible to talk because words would have been blatantly superfluous. Some male members of the species think that the way to have a certain power over a woman whom they do not feel comfortable with is to put them in a quasi-sexual context and this was what was starting to happen. Mickey, the boatman was a reassuring influence as he quietly fixed the engine.

When we arrived at Tieke we found Larry and Ma and everyone else bar a few teenagers getting ready to leave by the boat we arrived in. Rangi and I were thus left alone, in charge of the young people and guests who came down the river in canoes and would arrive at Tieke on dark in time for dinner. Ma said I could use their makeshift home and sleep in their bed while they were in town, which was quite a luxury and having the space to myself proved to be essential in the days and nights that followed. Because of the deep nature of our spiritual connection and interests, Rangi and I could be very close friends at times, and it started off that way, but there was always the zing in the air, which that polarity created and which was always potentially explosive. We were very similar in many ways and had I been in a male body things could have worked out well socially, but the Eagle would not have met the Serpent and I was about to find out just how deep and complex this energetic feat would be. Together we cleaned up the kitchen and cooked dinner for the three teenagers who kept out of our way as they too found Rangi rather tetchy, so they told me.

A young Israeli couple arrived by canoe and were fascinated by all that Rangi had to tell them about the Maori *wairua,* or spirituality. Rangi drew a comparison between the Israelis' desire for their promised land and the Maoris' desire to reclaim their homeland of Aotearoa. Both races had come from afar to settle in the place they had dreamed about and which they called home. All was peaceful that first night.

Rangi and I stayed up late talking amicably in front of the fire as we had much in common and he was genuinely interested in what I had to say. I knew I was in the company of someone who would not be surprised by or defensive about anything I had to say about earth energies or spiritual transmissions. Like many of the Maori people I met, deep spiritual connection was a way of life to him; everything was symbolic and had meaning, everything had consciousness in varying degrees. I gave him the stone with the Mayan features, which I had found up the river. The elders had told me the stone was an Ancestor, and it was an Ancestor who inspired fear in Rangi for some reason. I told him the story of Mantatjara's grandmothers' stone and the lizard, which spoke to me of the connection with the Mayans and the Wanganui River, and that I had been asked by spirit to acknowledge her in return by giving her a crystal skull and how that had come about. I also showed him the photograph of the white rainbow taken at *Huruharama* as well as the carving with the two birds found by the river and a white feather, which had come with me from Australia. He asked me what the white feather meant to me and I told him that to me it signified peace, unity and coming together. To him, it meant end of *mahi,* or 'spiritual' work in this case. I was to remember these words in dire circumstances later on.

The following day the Israeli couple left. A tremendous thunder and lightening storm broke and the river rose high allowing no other tourists access to Tieke. That meant, of course, that Rangi and I were thrown together with only the teenagers for distraction. Again we talked reasonably amicably and went about the daily work together.

By this time I had conveyed to him every detail of the messages I had received from spirit regarding him and it was very, very clear that I was not inventing it as he had been shown all the signs that had been prophesied would come about – the stone, the white feather, the white rainbow and the carving. It seemed to me that the journey to the cave would be made the following day without any trouble. Again we talked well into the night, in front of the log fire, amicably at first. Then I became apprehensive when the conversation started to become too familiar and there was a change in the energy. I stood up quickly and filled my hot water bottle from the urn, saying I would see him in the morning. He followed me out into this night of the dark moon, brandishing a lighter. He said he would light the way for me, as I would not be able to see where I was going. I argued that I would but when he flicked the lighter switch again I was facing the trunk of a *ponga* tree. These tree ferns grow taller in New Zealand than they do in Australia due to the lack of tall gum trees around them. One can always feel the loving or mischievous presence of the Ancestors around them. "See," he said, and followed me into my bedroom. There he saw a candle and lent over the bed to light it, remarking that Larry and Ma had a very comfortable bed and he did not like sleeping on the floor where he was in his tent. He also said he didn't have a candle. Starting to panic I gave him an extra candle I had in my bag and said goodnight. I am not sure to this day what was going on as my mission had nothing to do with physical relationships and I doubt very much if Rangi would have compromised himself in this way. I can only assume he was testing to see if he could get power over me in this way and was enraged by the rejection. He stormed out of the tent and I heard him sit down outside, so close I could still hear his breathing in the still night air.

I lay as still and silently as I could, inwardly calling to the Pleiadian family saying, "You'd better get me out of this." and I could hear their reassuring laughter. Sleep was not on the agenda as I was on the alert for anything. I now felt more strongly than ever that something archetypal was going on and Rangi and I were merely instruments so I stood back as it were to observe the situation from a distance. We had a black moon, an owl was hooting incessantly, the river was in flood and still rising, I started menstruating – for the last time as it happened – and an enraged Maori warrior was posted somewhere outside my flimsy dwelling.

It was 2 a.m. on my clock when out of the silence came a thunderous crash, screams, swearing, pleading and whimpering. My body went rigid and stayed that way until morning. My relationship with Rangi from this day on had become a full-blown challenge.

The previous night, apparently, the young people had got up out of bed and gone into the boatshed to sniff petrol. Rangi, who was lying in wait, for them or me, whichever manifested, I suppose, crashed a large wooden block down in front of the boys terrifying them, which accounted for the screaming and crying while they were being sworn at.

The young people kept even further out of the way yet they would try to find me alone to ask me questions about people close to them who had died. Word had got around that I could contact those who were beyond the veil. I had been dubbed the 'Witch' which, said with a strong New Zealand accent, sounded quite amusing.

Sometimes they would want to know how they could give up drugs or smoking, or just want to talk about their life and the problems, which had sent them to Tieke. Some of them wanted me to take them to the *urupa* to see if their Ancestors buried there wanted to help and talk to them. I was so in tune with the Ancestors and spirit of the land that these connections came easily to me. The young people remained terrified of Rangi and asked me if I was scared he would hit me.

That evening Rangi and I sat opposite each other at one of the long dining tables, most definitely in opposition. The polarities had set in and the Serpent and Eagle were locked into each other's energy. I felt an enormously powerful golden eagle over-lighting me and at the same time could see a dark and powerful ancestor standing behind Rangi. Once again Rangi instructed me on some of the more complex issues of Maori spirituality. It is a beautiful system of advanced and far-reaching knowledge. However, it was beyond me to absorb it in the circumstances and every time I said so I was told to shut up and listen with a thumping of fist on the table. At times I would compare what he was saying to my own understanding and experience. This was the Eagle trying to entice the Serpent to meet halfway but I was unceremoniously told to f——ng shut up. I was reduced to telling him to shut up for a change. I told him he was arrogant and a chauvinist pig and everything else bad I could think about yet I was no match for the Serpent jealously guarding his land. The whites of Rangi's eyes were now red and at times he was thumping the table with great force as the energies of the Ancestor activated in him. I was determined not to let him overpower me and it was only later that I realised, from the archetypal standpoint, that the Serpent would never come up and meet the Eagle halfway. The Serpent demands that the Eagle descends to the lowest point where he is curled up waiting. Then he knows that you can truly understand his position and are worthy of his trust. Only then will he condescend to rise up along with you. It gave me the understanding of how a deeply hurt and disempowered tribal person can move through the barrier between himself and an Anglo-Saxon. There is no other way, however good the intention. "Is this supposed to be an initiation or what?" I asked, and Rangi stood up clapping and cheering.

That night we again sat down next to each other in front of the hearth. We shared photographs and talked of skulls and the conversation veered back and forth between friendly and caustic. I brought up the subject of my main interest in being there but he said he could not possibly go into the wilderness with me because people would talk. He told me I was very humble and had a beautiful spirit but if he were to go with me I would need to meet with all the elder custodians of the middle reaches, who numbered about nine, and seek their approval. There was to be a meeting with them at Tieke in a couple of days. I was more than happy to wait since I knew these people and they were sympathetic to what I had to say. Coming from spirit these people could relate to my purpose and although it may have been outside their experience they could see no harm in anything I was being asked to do.

Rangi was still generally dictating to me as well as shouting violently sometimes and I was continuing to argue with him well into the night. Every now and again one of the teenage boys would get out of bed and run past us to ask if I was alright and the next day they were cheering and congratulating me on having good answers for Rangi. The only trouble was that the Eagle was not getting the picture, which would have made things a lot easier. I was ready to strangle him when I went to bed that night.

These few days had taken their toll. The Maori people for generations have used the power of the curse to keep adversaries at bay and I could constantly feel this energy levelled at me from the ancestor and coming through Rangi. So much so that I was continually running down to the river to cleanse myself and would go into the forest and lie down exhausted, my body shaking all over. Rangi watched my every move. Wherever I was I saw him watching.

That night I lay down in bed and I'd had it; so much so that instead of calling down the Pleiadian energy to me I left my body to join them in their spirit realm. There was much good humour there but when I said I could not work with this arrogant man and asked if I could go alone or have another, I was told there was no replacement. It was Rangi's privilege to take me there. The Ancestor in this cave we were being asked to visit was ready to work with him and would take him onto a different platform of understanding. This Ancestor had a very gentle but strong nature similar I was told to the inside of a whale's skull. To explain this they reminded me that I was seeing arrogance in Rangi while he was telling me I had great humility. They told me to look at this mirror image: arrogance – humility. The two are opposed but the greatest humility is like the inside of a whale's skull, which I then experienced and understood more of what was being shown to me. They reminded me of who I was and why I had come to this planet at this time. In fact, they showed me my whole journey to the end, which is just as well or I may have faltered along the way wondering whether it wouldn't be easier to pursue a conventional career.

The following morning I awoke determined to keep on an even keel with Rangi no matter how stringently I was provoked. However, it was not long before that notion fell by the wayside. After breakfast I had gone to sit quietly on a strategically placed bench on the bank looking up the river. I had not been there long when I heard a voice from above and behind the bench saying, "Speak." I said I had nothing to say unless we could meet on equal terms. The Eagle was still determined to get the Serpent to come up and meet it halfway, as I had not worked out that part yet. He announced that we were speaking on equal terms. I said that I did not think so as he was standing over me, talking down to me and there was a barrier between us, which was physically as well as metaphorically accurate. He said he knew where the cave was as he had taken a dinghy up the river the day before and had seen a red light shining on a cliff above the cave. He still wanted more details about what I had been told by spirit. I repeated all that I had been told for the umpteenth time. Then he wanted to know if I worked with the Light, if I was Pure and how did I know that it was that Ancestor who was communicating with me. I didn't know how I knew, I just knew and was completely exhausted with his questions, so again the relationship deteriorated. If this was breaking the barriers between the Celtic race and the Maoris because they were easier, I hated to think what was in store for me with the Aborigines!

CHAPTER 16

The Ra in the Mountains

A message had come through the radio transmitter that my son in Australia was in hospital with a fractured skull following a road accident. After talking at such depth about skulls it seemed that this was connected and I left for Wanganui on the jet boat when it arrived that day. In Wanganui I telephoned to my friend who had been looking after my children. My son was in intensive care and could have brain damage. As is my practice, I lay down quietly and tuned into my son's injury. Gradually I saw the dark patch around the left side of his head lighten until it looked as if it had fully healed. Seeing this I realised I did not have to return in a hurry. Instead, I typed a letter of request to all the custodians of the river and gave it to Ma who later told me none of them had any problem with me working with Rangi.

I felt extremely saddened by what had happened at Tieke, far beyond a personal sadness. It seemed as if many in spirit were expressing their sorrow all around me. Those Rangi had confided in saw that behind the arrogance there were many fears. On one occasion he told me that he was afraid of moving too fast and losing his family. He said he had to work with his people at their level, which he obviously thought was not very advanced.

As I understood it, the Ancestor who wanted to work with and teach Rangi had a very powerful but gentle nature, very unlike the one presently working with him. This would allow him to move with the times. Changing the frequency of the cave would affect those living and working within its resonance. Rangi was being called to guide this transition in a new way.

The Maori people work very closely with their Ancestors. They say that when they die only their body leaves but their spirit is still there with them as usual. A man in his thirties may suddenly express himself as a carver having had no training whatsoever but the inheritance from the Ancestor would have suddenly been triggered at a given point in time. Ancestral carvings often transmit a great deal of knowledge to the recipient and are treated with a great deal of respect. The elders were worried about the dark energies Rangi worked with and invited me up to a spiritual meeting in the mountains to revitalise my energy. This was just what I needed and I was privileged to be amongst some of the very strong people of the older generation. At the dining table I sat next to a lady in her nineties who was eating a full bowl of the New Zealand equivalent of live witchetty grubs and with much laughter she tried to encourage me to have some. Later, at the sleeping house this old lady stood up and spoke with such power that although my understanding of the Maori language was limited I felt captivated by the strength of her delivery. A very old man sitting at the table on my other side asked what I had been doing with Rangi – news had travelled – and when I told him he laughed and said, "It would take a woman with Rangi." He told me he knew that cave and the Ancestor I was talking about. These little gems always reassured me that I was not going mad and making the whole thing up at times.

At the same meeting a mother stood up to share her despair at a curse, which had been put on her family for seven generations by a jealous Ancestor. This was not unusual but brought devastation to the families affected. Some time ago the curse had activated in her daughter who was 21 years old. An otherwise very beautiful, talented and gentle person, when affected she would reach for the kitchen knife or some other weapon and try to kill her mother. As the daughter in this state was very strong and determined, the mother had lived through many traumatic attacks and her daughter would then spend some time in an institution. Recently her 17-year-old son had had his first attack with similar consequences and the mother was saying she had come to the end of the road and did not know where to turn, as nobody had been able to help her much as they had tried. She shared with all there that she had had a dream recently where the wallpaper in her room was peeling off layer by layer until a photograph of her aunt Isabel was revealed. Isabel told her to take her children to the healing pools nearby, to enter the water and ask for healing of the spirit. As she was talking, my eyes became fixated on the eyes of a young girl sitting next to her, much to my embarrassment, as the girl became aware of this and was feeling awkward. However, my eyes would not leave hers until the curse came out from her and flew at me, like an orange/red flaming wind. It tried to enter my being but eventually recoiled. I quietly shared this and my experiences of being in the healing pools with the mother when we were alone and she said she was very afraid of the power of the pools and wanted my reassurance that she had been given a healing message. I said I felt she had been empowered knowing that there was a way she could take charge of the situation. Later, when I met her at a Marae meeting she told me she had taken her children to the pools and things had improved.

At night Alvin and I sat outside under the moon, looking over the snowy mountain tops of Pihanga and Tongariro and enjoyed the great beauty and vitality this land has to offer.

CHAPTER 17
Meeting the Mountains

After a short stay back in Australia, I returned to New Zealand and made my way up to Tieki then to the home of Larry and Ma in Raetihi. I had been told I would be working with the mountain of Ruapehu when the volcano erupted as I was connecting with the salamander energy both in water and fire within the earth. We slept well that night and in the morning I arose and went to sit on their front veranda. A thick mist clouded whatever view was before me but as the sun rose the mist gently lifted to reveal the great snow-covered mountain right in front of me. This surprised me, as I had had no idea where Ruapehu was. I ask the elders whether Ruapehu had erupted recently and was told that the last time was about 50 years previously. I told them that I thought it would erupt again before long because of the spiritual message I had received.

Arriving back in Wanganui, Martha, Alvin, Erina and I decided to take a tent and visit Taranaki Mountain. We made beautiful connections with the spiritual essence of the place and bathed in the three Maori healing pools at the base of three waterfalls. At night we sat in a small trampers' hut and lit candles. Three of us sat around a table and felt compelled to invoke the Ancestor who was holding onto Rangi with such determination. He duly turned up and the door of the hut flew open with a great gust of wind, which managed to extinguish most of the candles. This was an Ancestor who had many regrets about his life and the way he had treated his family, so he was not yet at peace and willing to go to the light although his time had come. We thanked him for the great work he had done as custodian of the land and talked his concerns through with him until he was finally at peace and disappeared into a column of light that we had purposefully created for him.

CHAPTER 18
Matahiwi Ra

There was a deep connecting energy forming between Glastonbell and Tieke at this time. In previous years several people connected with Glastonbell, and committed to working with the geomancy of the land, had travelled to many sacred areas in Aotearoa. They were called at appropriate times to work with the energies in specific ways and a strong link had already been established between the two places. The door to the Wanganui River, land and people had been opened to those who were seeking a deeper connection, by my first going there. Now a diverse group of about a dozen people were asked to participate in a spiritual gathering, a *Ra,* at Matahiwi Marae, by members of the Ponga family who were followers of the prophet Ratana.

The *Ra* is held annually at Matahiwi as well as at other locations throughout the year. Like any Maori gathering, the guests were called onto the Marae in the traditional way, only when the woman's *karanga* filled the air. This haunting sound jolted one into the present and as each guest approached the line of hosts to receive the heartfelt greetings there would be few dry eyes. The families took part in these spiritual gatherings to heal them from a harsh past as well as to come together to share food and stories, as they have always done. Each person would stand in a circle and share what they were feeling or what difficulties they were experiencing. The presence of their Ancestors could always be felt strongly and sometimes they were mischievous, upsetting people. At other times an overwhelming energy of love would come into the *whare* and I was constantly surprised by the words that came forth when I stood up to speak, as if my Ancestors were guiding my speech, as well as my footsteps and actions for the occasion. It was a great learning as well as healing experience for many. Tribal conflicts were brought out into the open unashamedly and dealt with as best they could and the eating experience was always a joyful one.

By this time the Maori women and others who had been engulfed in inflammatory feelings about the *Pakeha,* which included me, had worked out the difficulties that certain individuals among them were creating. Several had asked me to help them understand the self-healing process and I had shared with them any techniques I knew and helped them work with these where I could. They were coming a long way with their healing in a very short time despite a heavy past.

During the three days of my time there I spoke only briefly to Rangi, whom I hoped would join me up the river at Tieke this time. He did not, much to my chagrin – thrice asked by spirit to make a particular journey and thrice refusing was serious. I knew for sure that the request had come from those beyond the veil and not from me but he maintained he had his doubts about that.

Standing by the river at Matahiwi the night before we were to leave, I looked across the water and saw a column of bright light descend from the sky down to meet the summit of the grassy peak across the water. I was being asked to go there at the Maori New Year when the Pleiades rose again in the sky. The following morning a friend drove us to the jet boat at Pipiriki.

CHAPTER 19
The Tirahoiwaka

It was one of those very still days with water in the river, clear as glass. Beautiful intricate carvings can be seen all along the banks of the river on a day like this – patterns from an ancient past looked like the work of Gods. There is a scientific explanation for this, as there is for most things, but most things also are imbued with spiritual content or creative intelligence. The Maoris say that when conditions are just right and these carvings appear strongly to the traveller, it is the Ancestors welcoming the guest to their land. It is interesting that some people just do not and cannot see them for the life of them.

As usual we had a most peaceful time at Tieke with Larry and Ma and much laughter despite, as well as at the expense of, the political situation and characters involved. A few of the friends from the *Ra* joined us there. It was summertime and the weather was warm and sunny. The river was flowing fast and we would jump in from as far up the bank as we could, letting the current carry us downstream at high speed.

Families had gathered to meet the people coming down the river in canoes on the *Tirahoiwaka*. This was a grand annual event, which many of all ages tried to make, challenging the rapids all the way down to Tieke and beyond and camping overnight at the various stops along the way. The elders would tell the people all the stories they knew about the history of different stops along the river, where the old *pas* had been, who had lived there and what events had taken place.

Several tourists were camping at Tieke, among them a musician and her partner from Germany. They asked me if I would take them for a walk through the forest and up the hill to the *urupa*, or graveyard, as they were interested in what they had learned from talking to the Maori people. We went up there and lay on the ground next to each other in meditation to connect with the land. From deep within the earth I saw a Celtic stone spiral rise up from the ground to meet a Maori wooden spiral coming down from the heavens. Again I was learning about a connection between the Celtic and the Maori people and experiencing the energetic union of the two spirals. I shared this with my two companions, whom I felt had contributed to the connecting energies and although they did not have this experience they had tears in their eyes from the enormous love they felt come into our space as we were lying there.

Back at base I saw a young Maori friend whom I knew to be interested in the traditions and I asked him what the spiral meant to the Maori people. He directed me towards a man next to him who had carvings, or *moko*, as far up his very short shorts as one could see as well as on his face and arms. He was a master carver who had arrived with the *Tirahoiwaka* group and had all the arrogance that any warrior master carver could possibly have. We called him the Greek God for obvious reasons. I was in the position of having to direct my question to him, although in other circumstances he would not have been one I would have approached on such a subject. With nose in the air he told me he could not possibly discuss such a sacred matter when he was having a cup of tea and I was to see him later. I wondered what the difference between us was that allowed me to speak of sacred matters, but prevented him, while having a cup of tea.

I became a challenge for him from then on. When I did not approach him again after his cup of tea, he sat down next to me nearly knocking me off my seat. He sat opposite me as if reading a newspaper but looking across above it. He stood in front of me, so closely that the heel of his shoe was on the toe of mine.

Later, I was to find that there are many ancient Maori laws, as is customary and was necessary in any tribal situation in the past, which are based around a concept of *tapu*. Tapu covers many things and like most Maori words can only be translated as a concept not a particular word. It can mean sacred, untouchable, forbidden and many other things. It was explained to me that having a cup of tea after the formalities of coming onto a Marae took the *tapu* off a guest and his reasoning could have been something loosely associated with this.

However, there was somehow a turnaround for this man during his stay at Tieke, where the elders peppered their wisdom with a dash of humility. In his parting speech the elders translated for me his words of apology for his attitude on arrival, saying he had learnt humility during his stay with the people at Tieke.

I was to witness this warrior arrogance coupled with vulnerability quite often in New Zealand and one has to really delve into the history of the Maori warrior for a fuller understanding of the strengths and frailties of this role in current society.

My purpose at this time was to wait for Rangi in the hope that he would turn up to complete this work we were to do together. I was concerned, as the energies that I was carrying indicated the time was imminent. However, he did not turn up so I waited for the next communication from the spiritual realms of how events were to unfold.

One night while standing outside the sleeping area, observing the clear night sky, I looked across the river where the Pleiades were flickering as usual and noticed they were appearing and disappearing and dancing with great vitality. It was so unusual that I brought a few friends out to watch them and they were not disappointed. In my tent I was still wide awake well into the night when I suddenly heard ancient Maori chanting coming up from beneath the ground. The memory of years of chanting had been imprinted in the ground. Later, the family told me there had once been an old Marae where I felt the sound had originated. The chanting went on and on for hours as I drifted into a deep trance. In this state a Maori warrior in spirit appeared in front of me. His face was covered with intricate *moko*, or tattoos. First I was shown images of black rocks in dark, grey water, followed by a flock of brilliantly white birds flying up around the rocks out of the water, with which the sun shone brightly and a rainbow appeared. The warrior said to me, "I want to come with you to the waterfall tomorrow to meet the spirit of the Rainbow People." With that, I fell into a deep sleep until morning.

The next morning, having no idea where this waterfall was, I took a different route up to the *urupa*. As I quietly stood on a ridge, overlooking a creek, I became aware of the sound of distant rushing water down to my right. It seemed like a long and arduous hike to get there. When I returned to base I told the elders what had been happening and asked if there was a waterfall in this direction. Larry said there was such a waterfall known as *tapu* to them as children.

Ma understood the rainbow as her people were the people of the rainbow and she came from an area along the river known as the Rainbow Valley where rainbows were often seen upside down, on their side, straight up and down, circular and any other shape imaginable. I showed her the photograph of the white rainbow I had taken at Waiwai's place in the hills at Jerusalem. She asked me what the white rainbow meant to me and I told her for me it meant people of different tribes coming together. For her it meant death. In hindsight, it could have meant both.

CHAPTER 20

The Thunderbird meets the Eel

A friend and I set off for the waterfall in the direction of the spot where I had found the stone with the Mayan face some years previously. This stone had communicated with me that it wanted me to take it home to Australia for a while and bring it back later. I had picked it up spontaneously while sitting on a rock where the river meets the creek and now it was telling me to return via the creek junction to get to the waterfall. This took us considerably out of our way, especially as the river was in flood and a strong current was pushing against us as we made our way up the slippery banks, occasionally having to walk in waist deep water to get to the guardian's stronghold at the junction. Luckily, when involved with earth energy work one is given extra powers and we made it without too much trouble. We then had to make our way along the swollen creek, mostly finding it easier to walk up the middle of it than attempt to travel by the steep, muddy, banks. This was a case of climbing over many rocks and fallen tree trunks.

I came across a large stone in shallow water, which obviously held the spirit of another Ancestor. It was rounded with a scaly back and had the perfect, detailed features and shape of a fish. It is not at all unusual in the Maori world to meet Ancestors in rocks, stones, bones, sticks and anywhere in fact. The land is so alive with their spirit and is often extremely loving and warm. As with many things connected with the Maori, the heart is opened wide when connecting with this energy. We were almost at our destination when my friend fell and slid down a bank of mud towards the creek. As she was scraped and bruised we decided to make an ally of the enemy and covered ourselves completely with the mud. This worked and we arrived at the opening to the cave without further drama.

We were wearing bathers and were camouflaged by mud. The sky had a covering of heavy grey, watery clouds and the entrance to the cave consisted of cold, dark water with high rock formations on both sides that almost touched at the top adding to the gloom. The *kaitiaki,* or guardians of the cave stood out to greet us.

It is a strange thing with the land, how its energy folds in on itself if there is no one there who can recognise it and acknowledge it, just like humanity. For those who are sensitive enough, it is a matter of approaching quietly with respect and appreciation and the energies of the land will open up with all their might and joy.

At the entrance there was a large Whale on the left hand side and a large Eel on the right. After acknowledging these two awesome guardians and communicating my purpose I felt that I could continue with their blessing. I progressed slowly forward, as there were many Beings of all shapes, sizes and forms on both sides of the high rocks to be acknowledged before the granting of their permission to continue would come. Working at this depth of connection with the spirit of the land, one's feet would be held firm as if in concrete until the permission came and the doors opened, then the feet would move forward spontaneously without needing to think about it. All the time, the water was getting deeper, blacker and colder. The cave was at the back of this dark area ahead of me. When I was almost unable to keep my feet on the ground any more and just about suffering from hypothermia, from out of the black pool ahead of me emerged a large black sacred Eel and at the same moment I looked up to my right, over a short waterfall and up another towering gully to a very long, slim waterfall. From that waterfall I saw a rainbow coloured Thunderbird fly down its entire length, through the gully, in through the crown of my head and out of my heart to meet the rising Eel. At that I turned around and sought the entrance to this cavern as fast I as I could to release by chilled bones. At the water's edge I threw a small stone, which had been brought from a sacred area in New South Wales, Australia, into the Eel's domain. As it hit the water, sparkles rose up around the dark walls and the sun finally came out from behind a cloud lighting up the whole area and bringing warmth. It was like the vision I had been shown the night before of the dark rocks and clouds, illuminated by the white birds flying up around them.

It is always very satisfying to know that spiritual work of this nature has been accomplished successfully and despite the fact that Rangi did not come, spirit had found a way around it. We returned exhausted but exhilarated to the Marae at Tieke where a hot cup of tea was waiting as usual, but we were called outside to look at two very bright double rainbows reaching out across the land and forests from the waterfall area to Tieke Marae. This was seen as an acknowledgement from the spirits of the rainbow people and confirmation that we had reached completion of this part of the journey.

CHAPTER 21

The White Feather

The following day on my way to the *urupa,* I looked across the creek towards the trees and notice two balls of light flashing from two separate places, high up the slopes but not quite at the summit and knew that I was now being asked to go up there. I stayed at Tieke for a few more weeks hoping that my alleged co-worker would eventually turn up, as this was really difficult terrain. Having little sense of direction and not the best with heights, especially wet, muddy ones, I was sure to get lost if I went alone. Once again I asked the spiritual realms if I could have another guide but again was told there was no replacement so reluctantly I set off alone. I took some water, a sandwich, and light sleeping bag with me as this trip had an unusually foreboding air about it. In fact, in my normal state of being I would never have attempted it.

I made the ascent much quicker than I had imagined stopping where I thought I had seen the first ball of light. Then continuing, after a short meditation, up the slope to where I had seen the second ball of light. Here I was told that I had mistakenly already passed the second point some way back. I continued onwards realising I was probably hopelessly lost, unhappy now about my co-worker's absence.

Several hours later finding myself meeting steep bluffs at every turn and realising I was miles away from where I had made my ascent, I spread out my sleeping bag, ate my sandwich and prepared to spend the night there, damp though it was. It was also getting a bit late in the day to think about returning. I closed my eyes and sat quietly when much to my surprise I heard the rush of water falling from a great height. I was actually sitting directly above the waterfall where I had seen the Thunderbird. That brightened my outlook considerably as it gave me my bearings and I was beginning to think that this journey had its meaning, as always, after all.

As I looked between my feet I noticed a pure white bird's feather. "Great," I thought jokingly, "End of *mahi.* I can go home now," believing that there was little hope of that, but a frantic rustling to my right made me turn and look. Invisible hands were parting the stems and grasses of the undergrowth, exposing a wide pathway. Incredulously I walked over to where this was happening and saw that a track was being created all the way down to the creek. From there I knew my way home and had just enough time to reach the creek on dark. The others were having dinner when I returned and Larry introduced me to the newly arrived guests, saying, "And that thing that just walked out of the bush is Anne".

CHAPTER 22
The Urupas

With my task completed I could have returned home but chose to stay on and for a change, have a holiday and experience Tieke in my normal state of being.

During this time the bones of an ancestral woman, whose burial place had been dug up by council to make a new road, were returned to Tieke to find their final resting place. The family there did not know precisely where to bury them and in their usual caring way wanted the outcome to be spiritually correct. They turned to me and asked me if I knew where they were to go but I had no idea. They said that I may have a dream about it that night and probably had received guidance to that effect because generally speaking I do not have prophetic or even interesting dreams. That night I did dream. The old lady came to me and with her bones cupped in her hands she said, "The body decays but the spirit stays forever. My spirit abides in the miro tree." I communicated my message to the family the following morning and solemnly we all made our ascent to the *urupa*. There is, in fact, an ancient miro tree close to the entrance to the *urupa* and we stood in a circle beside it for further guidance. Everyone looked at me and I was told there was someone in the circle who knew where to go and before I finished talking Ma was on her way to a cluster of ponga trees where another Ancestor had been buried many years ago.

The following day another member of the family asked if I would come across the river with her in the dinghy to the *urupa* where her parents were buried on their family property and we spent the whole day at this peaceful place.

Next morning I left on the jet boat for Pipiriki. Rangi and my other Wanganui friends were to be at Matahiwi Marae that weekend, running a children's creativity workshop, so they came and collected me. I learned to weave earrings in the shape of the Baskets of Knowledge in dark and light flax and enjoyed spending time with the children.

I told Rangi about my journey and he looked devastated. It was then that I noticed his spirit had left him and he might not stay much longer in this world, which would be a great loss for the people. It is not unusual that when someone chooses not to follow the next step of their spiritual pathway when it is presented that they will choose instead to leave the earth. It put me in a very unenviable place but I felt I had done everything within my power to reassure him that the direction was coming from the highest realms of the spiritual kingdom and there was nothing to be feared.

Again I was asked to join members of the family to take the canoes across the river to the Matahiwi *urupa*. Once again this was a most peaceful and loving place but I asked the spirits there why I had been taken to three different *urupas* in so many days. They told me it was because some of the old people wanted to make a last connection with the people of the land before they left them for other realms. They said they had stayed around until they felt the land to be safely back in their family's custodianship.

In New Zealand the Maori Ancestors would appear to me as old women dressed in black with short white hair and behind each would stand a very tall figure with the head of a bird and body of a human like the Egyptian Toth figure. The Maori people do recite their genealogy, or *whakapapa,* back through Egyptian times.

CHAPTER 23

Night Owls on the East Coast of Australia

On returning to Australia I travelled with Martha up the east coast, visiting Lorraine and Elaine Williams, the sisters of Lucy, the Aboriginal lady we had met at Pakaitore. We stayed at Glastonbell for a while and Martha contacted her Maori Ancestors in several places along the way. Many Maoris had found their way to Australia in the distant past as well as the present.

A friend from the Wanganui River told me a story of when she left her homeland the one and only time. She had hoped to visit an uncle whose address had been given to her. However, arriving at Bondi Beach she found that the uncle was not at home and the place looked deserted. Unsure of what to do next, she returned to Central Station and sat on one of the benches across from an old Aboriginal man who was sitting alone. They both sat there for some time until she went over and sat down next to him. He asked her if she knew she was sitting above the bones of her Ancestors and told her some history. My friend told him her story and he said that if she would trust him she could come on the train with him to his homeland. She did this and when they arrived in Woollongong she did what the Maoris usually do when they visit someone. She bought a large box of food thinking they were close to home. The old man asked her to follow him and they walked a long way until they reached the bush. Following a track through the bush, he in front, she behind and the box getting heavier by the minute, no words were spoken until he asked her to look at the back of his head until he told her to stop, as they continued through the bushland. She felt a strange energy here but once out of it they were in a clearing and home. My friend had expected to find several families of the old man's tribe here but there was only one medicine man in his camp near the entrance to the clearing. He smudged her with smoking gum leaves to cleanse her from the city's energies and she continued on a little further with the other old man. For six months she lived as they did, without many words being spoken. At the end of this period, however, the old man said you can go now and took her back to the medicine man, who asked her which tribe she was from. When she told him it was the Ngati Ruru, or Night Owl tribe, the old man confirmed that he thought so, as his people were also of that tribe, the Doonooch.

Martha and I also went to visit members of the Doonooch Tribe at Wreck Bay who had travelled over to Tieke and been hosted by the Ponga families. I felt the Night Owl was part of my connection to these people too. From my days in Scotland I always remembered owls being around my mother, bringing more often than not, gloomy tidings. In more recent times owls had been entering my environment more and more, especially on the days preceding an intended trip to Aotearoa. One day before leaving for New Zealand, a friend and I were sitting having a cup of tea on the veranda in the National Park. We had taken shelter from the sudden downpour and looked up to a tall tree close by to see an enormous owl sitting blinking in the rain. In this region we were used to seeing the powerful owl, which is also large but this one was two or three times that size. My friend could feel its vibration doing something to her as he just sat and blinked at us. I am well used to spirit birds appearing at odd times but I thought I would confirm with one of the park rangers that this was not in fact a powerful owl. Soon all the rangers and staff came out from the office and confirmed that they had never seen anything like it. At least they saw it, as often in situations like this, people will say, "What owl?"

CHAPTER 24
The Placenta and Tamahaki Meeting

My next trip to New Zealand included a special mission. I had to take through customs the placenta of a Maori baby who had just been born in the Blue Mountains of Sydney and return it to the priest at its family Marae at Ranana along the old Wanganui River road with which I am so familiar. The placenta of course had to be kept on ice and there was a certain urgency to get it to its destination.

I stayed with friends, Christine and Ross Wallis at Ohakune, who were to attend a Tamahaki meeting in Raetihi the following day. A meeting of the Tamahaki tribe was in progress when we arrived and I was happy to see so many friends together. The meeting had its usual melee of arguments and angry outbursts but also the positive, friendly sharing of ideas and circumstances. The Tamahaki people of the middle reaches of the river were still experiencing intense times, attending endless meetings with the Department of Conservation whose mission was to exercise control over their lands and river.

I asked someone when the Maori New Year was as I had been directed to go to the peak at Matahiwi "at the time of the Maori New Year when the Pleiades rise in the sky." They directed me to Wiremu, who had come down in support, from the tribe of Maniopoto in the Waikato region. It had been suggested to me by some that I should visit the ancient Star Temple and House of Learning at Te Miringa de Kakara and I had taken note but placed it aside until it happened. Wiremu invited me to stay at his place and visit this Temple, which was in the region where he lived. As, for the first time, my return ticket left from Hamilton, close to his home rather than Wellington. This seemed like it would be an appropriate time to visit the Temple.

Ross suggested that Christine and I take their truck and drive to the Marae where the placenta had to be buried. There was deep snow all along the river road, which could be treacherous at the best of times with landslides narrowing it down to the width of a large vehicle in places. The truck fizzled out along the way and neither Christine nor I knew the first thing about how to fix it but eventually help arrived and we met the priest and his wife at Ranana. They were pleased to receive the placenta of the newly born baby, as their feeling is that the person will be drawn back to its Marae by the placenta being buried in the earth there beside the Ancestors. With spades and heavy boots we tramped across the snowy paddock to the *urupa* where prayers and blessings were said for the baby and the placenta was buried amongst its Ancestors.

According to a message received by me on a previous visit to *Aotearoa*, Ruapehu erupted, throwing molten ashes all over this region. The Maori people call Ancestor Ruapehu, *Koro,* or Grandfather and celebrated its activity and vitality, although those involved in farming and the ski industry did not. I stayed at Ross and Christine's farm during most of the mountain's erupting days, connecting strongly with the energy from the lounge or a high snowy ridge on the property, which was very close and almost within range of the lava flow. The air was filled with an eerie silence caused by the combination of the thick snow covering, ash and fire. We watched lumps of molten lava the size of a vehicle thrown skywards by day and night for several days until I returned to Wanganui, as it was time to visit the mountain at Matahiwi.

Chapter 25
Matahiwi Mountain

It was the time of the Maori New Year when the Pleiades rise in the sky again. Martha, Alvin, Erina and I visited Alvin's father to pick up a canoe before driving to Matahiwi. From there we crossed the river to the foot of the mountain, whose peak had been shown to me by a column of light striking it the previous year. Once again it was a long, barefoot, muddy climb to the top but with mud up to the knees, we eventually arrived at the top with camping gear and food for the night. My friends set up camp before nightfall while I scurried across the ridge to where I was being called. It turned out that there was a deep crater on the other side which was fairly inaccessible.

The forces that were working through me would often give me sounds to change a frequency and/or movements for the same reason. Generally I allowed these to arise spontaneously, hoping I was alone and not scaring anyone. On most occasions I was very much alone, as the places I was sent to were quite remote and usually involved a parabolic journey. On this occasion it started to rain, as often happens when I am performing such rituals. As it was getting dark I headed back quickly to our camp all cosily set up for a good night's sleep.

We all experienced a sleep-free night, being taken on a journey through different realms and meeting all kinds of characters. Even Alvin, who although very intuitive, never saw anything, saw quite a lot that night. There were probably all sorts of energetic and historic reasons for this visionary evening. I was told that for years the old Tohungas used to sit in a meditative circle up on the peak at the Maori New Year when the Pleiades rose in the sky again. I was also told by the elders that the crater was *tapu*. Consequently, when they hunted pigs in the region of the crater behind this mountain, if a dog ever went down there, it went mad. One old man who had been brought up in that region, told me he had found a huge gold nugget there as a child but had received such a scolding from his parents for being in the crater that it was never mentioned again.

We returned to Matahiwi Marae where we picked up our van and my friends drove me along the now very familiar river road to Pipiriki to wait for a boat to take me up to Tieke. Mickey had already left for Tieke to pick up some of the carvers who had been staying there, so I had dinner with the family and went to bed. It had rained continuously for several days – not unusual in New Zealand – and I felt damp and cold as I got into bed before drifting off into a very sound sleep.

Before long, however, I was awoken by people coming into my room looking for life jackets in the cupboard. Two good pig dogs had taken off when they were hunting on the river and the men were going to look for them. As the night wore on, however, things turned out to be very different. On the return journey from Tieke, the 'Tieke Lady' had spun out of control and hit a bank leaving everyone floundering in the freezing water. Although this had occurred in one of the most treacherous rapids on the river, most had managed to swim to shore where they stayed for several hours in the cold darkness until rescued. One young man, a strong swimmer, could not be found. There was hope that he had been carried further downstream and would eventually manage to emerge onto a bank.

The very experienced search parties went out that night and the days to come. The men knew the river and its moods intimately and came together in many canoes to search the river for the body, as hope soon faded of finding the young carver alive The women cooked hot meals constantly to keep their spirits up. In the evenings we all sat and prayed with the parents and family of the lost boy. Several days later the body was retrieved from the river where it had floated downstream to the town.

It was one of the saddest times I experienced on the river although there were many more to come. The weather, the atmosphere and the occasion had combined to exhaust everyone. Several people including myself had contracted flu. My Wanganui friends, sensing that I would be suffering, came unexpectedly to pick me up and take me up to Wiremu's at Te Kuiti, which was an enormous relief as the work had been done and I was feeling quite ill.

CHAPTER 26

The Star Temple – Te Miringa de Kakara

Once before these sad events at Wanganui, while walking along the riverbank in Wanganui, a brown hawk almost flew into my face to get my attention. I stood still to receive the message he was bringing. My hand was in my pocket holding the bone carving of the two birds at the time and I was told it was a time when the earth energies on the earth's grid between Wanganui and Te Miringa de Kakara, the Star Temple, were to be unblocked and unified.

The ancient Maori people had had in place a series of *pos*, or carved poles, which anchored the various river Maraes into the earth's power in particular positions, based on the wisdom of the Tohungas of the time. These river poles were linked into the *po* at the centre of the Cross House at Te Miringa, this being a major sacred place of the Maori people where the Tohungas of the past had come to learn their very advanced arts. It was said that the Star People had created the original house and a great deal of knowledge was imprinted in the land there in the centre of North Island.

When the young boy had originally handed the bone carving to me and I had felt the energy contained in it, I took it back to the house where Martha and I lay down and tuned into it. Together we were taken on a journey up the river from Wanganui past all the Maraes and *pos* along the river. I was travelling along the passageway of the inner earth and Martha on the earth's surface. Along the way we were both clearing anything obstructing our passage. On the surface Martha met with many of her Ancestors and would talk to them and heal their sorrows.

Alvin and Martha drove me to Te Kuiti where my main focus was to go to the Cross House at Te Miringa but on arrival at Wiremu's old house in the hills I became very ill with the flu bug I had contracted at Pipiriki. I took to my bed for several days while Wiremu enjoyed playing host to his guests from the river. When I recovered enough to join in the action, the others were preparing to return home to Wanganui.

Wiremu's tribal land was also very strong and filled with the spirit of the Ancestors. We walked to a nearby cave where his Ancestor, Maniopoto, had lived and it was very dark when I entered and walked towards what seemed to be a deep, sunken pool of water in front of me. After meditating there for a while, I opened my eyes and could see quite clearly now that I was accustomed to the darkness. I leant forward to look more closely at what looked like a white hand rising up out of the dark water below me and as I did so a giant white eagle flew up past me and out of the cave. Maniopoto was a Chief whose totem was the Black Eagle and this was the totem of that tribe. On another visit to this cave when looking across the water to a small ledge I saw a very old woman, a spinning wheel, a web and a large spider. The old woman said she was Maya spinning the illusion of life while the grandmother spider was also spinning her web. Rangi, who performed impeccably and taught the Maori art form of the Bird Dance, comprising thirteen different birds, had warned me not to get caught in the dance of the spider and perhaps I should have heeded his warning when I arrived at the Maniopoto stronghold. That night back at the house we received a visit from the two sisters who lived at Te Miringa saying that they had seen the white and black eagles flying together in the sky again.

Te Miringa de Kakara means something like the 'Fragrance of the Forest' but there are few trees there now as the land has been offered up to sheep farming. The remains of the ancient Temple are still there and a more recent house has been built next to it. The area is exposed to high winds as well as high energy and it was very cold on that first visit. I lay down on the grass in the cross house by what remained of the central pole and instantly felt the rush of clear energy as all the poles joined up from Wanganui. This was followed by the words, "Your work is done," which sounded good. I had broken the barrier between the Celtic and Maori race, doors had been opened, the Eagle had unified with the Serpent, the Thunderbird had unified with the Eel and the Poles had been unified along the grid, but it turned out that my work was far from finished in New Zealand if I was game enough to carry on.

The land around Te Kuiti is of limestone and is a lush green with underground waterways throughout. There are many caves and tomos, where one can look down far below the earth's surface and see water flowing. The limestone forms interesting shapes inside these caves with some very old stalagmites and stalactites, which have a life of their own in this netherworld. One particular stalagmite looks like one of the large cat family and rises from the ground of a cavern, like a watchful Being keeping

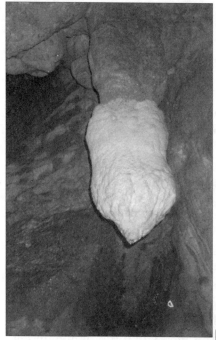

guard of his area. This was one that the Maori people regarded as sacred and it was said to be a transmitter of energy and information from the realm of Sirius. The stalactite above it was said to be the receiver of information for the Beings of Sirius. The Maoris, like all ancient races, communicated regularly with their star connections and this was not an easy place to get to as one had to climb up the face of a cliff, walk in the dark sideways along a narrow passage until it opened out into a larger area where the stalagmite had resided for many years. The passage continued on and occasionally one could look down through one of the limestone openings to see the river flowing below if one had a light. When I asked for information there I was told it connected to the other realm each year on May 22nd, when the energy for this bridge was at its most powerful.

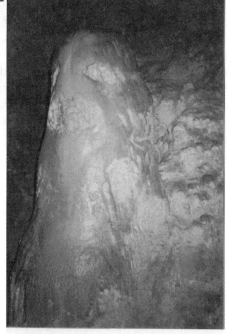

Right: Stalagmite - transmitter to Sirius.
Above: Stalactite - receiver from Sirius.

CHAPTER 27
Mangapapapa and Pureora Forest

My next stay in Australia centred on a property owned by a friend of mine close to the edge of the escarpment where previously we had experiences with the eagles and bones of the people who had been massacred there. Some local Aboriginal people had continued to meet there and we had become involved with their interests as they shared their stories and hopes with us. The older people's main concern was to help the Aboriginal youth to find direction in the modern world and also teach them their traditional ways. An elder, in his eighties, had taken us to the base of a mountain where in the old days the young boys were initiated. The boy would approach the area where a priest would be waiting with a large rock of gold, kept at the foot of the mountain for the initiation ceremonies. The boy would wait on the far side of the rock while the priest would break the boy's totem over the rock, allowing the blood to flow. The Priest would then rub his hands all over the gold and blood absorbing these two energies into his hands. He would climb the mountain and meditate with his hands held high towards the sky until they felt like fire. Then he would descend to the waiting boy and rub his hands all over the boy's shoulders to imbue him with his totemic energy. The boy was then free to marry and walk in another tribe's lands. In spirit I had been told that the Pleiadians connect through the blood and the Sirians the gold.

The local Aboriginal people were very interested to hear of how the Maori people were working with their youth and had their own preschools where the Maori language was taught and spoken from an early age. Not so long ago, as part of the disempowerment program, it was forbidden by law to speak the Maori language so a generation had to relearn it. Stan and Barry, two Aboriginal men from the east coast, particularly wanted to come over and meet the Maori elders.

There was to be a gathering of indigenous elders from around the world at Manu Ariki Marae near Te Kuiti later that year and Stan and Barry would come. Twelve friends in all decided to come over for the itinerary we offered and the strange thing was when we stood up on the Marae to share our backgrounds just about as many races were represented. We had a delegate from Germany, Denmark, Cherokee, Scotland, Africa,

Lebanon, Romany Gypsy, two Aborigines from Australia and three non-Aboriginal Australians. To me it was like the white rainbow promise of the tribes coming together. Not all followed the entire itinerary but most of us arrived in Wellington and were met at the airport by Alvin and Martha. After spending a few nights in Wanganui and visiting such places as Lake Taupo, we proceeded up the river road to Matahiwi Marae to join the gathering at the Ra. As always the traditional welcome overwhelmed most of the group and the Ra was a wonderful introduction into the Maori world. Rangi was friendly towards me now that the pressure was off but I regretted his inability to accept his part in the work, which I knew was not yet completed and he looked very unwell. Contacts and friendships were made and Stan and Barry, whom we were now calling Ban and Starry, were having a ball and were quite inspired by what they saw and learned. There was also the intensity of the healing and sharing in this high vibrational location, which caused a few dramas. From Matahiwi we carried on up the river road in our two minibuses to Pipiriki. From there we took the large jet boat up to Tieke and enjoyed a few restful days there before carrying on up the river to a Marae which is truly situated in unspoiled wilderness, and, like Tieke, can only be accessed by canoe or jet boat.

Mangapapapa is a very special place and this was a very special occasion. The resident family welcomed us onto the Marae in quite an austere manner balanced by the gentle singing of the women's waiata. The energy was intense and explosive and everyone's senses became fine tuned to fit the occasion. The presence of the Ancestral energy as well as the present Keepers of the land ushers one's attention rather rapidly into the present. We were told there had been bitter conflicts fought on this land, which may have partially accounted for the contrast between the feeling and expression of the place to the peace of Tieke. Throughout our stay there was tension in the air as well as very enjoyable moments with the music of guitars, didgeridoo and singing in the evenings. Again, we all slept on mattresses around the meeting house and by evening listened to the men stand up and speak in their tongue but translated for the overseas visitors at times. After this we went around the whole group allowing each person to share who they were, where they came from, their feelings about the river and the stay at Mangapapapa and anything else they felt moved to share. This was often very emotive as at these meetings great wounds from a distant past between the races would rear up to be healed, which is what the journey was about. It was further confirmation for me, if I still needed it, that the doors to a closer relationship had been opened and on leaving, the custodian of Mangapapapa told me in recognition and acknowledgement that I held the key. It really felt in the gathering of this larger group that the barriers between the Celtic race and the Maoris had indeed been broken and I left, feeling elated and much relieved.

Back at Pipiriki some of us got in a minibus and drove further north along the river road to Raetihi. This part of the road was extremely narrow in places due to mudslides caused in wet weather. On arrival at Te Kuiti people said they had never seen a white Aborigine before. Stan and Barry were sitting terrified in the back seat, not trusting that the universe was on our side. At Te Kuiti mattresses had been spread out next to each other around the disused railway waiting room. We did not get much sleep that night because of all the downtown action and the odd express train tearing past. As someone remarked in the morning, it was like sleeping in a railway station. Bright and early the following morning we were ushered off with tents and sleeping bags to spend ten days in Pureora Forest. This is truly an entrancing forest and I think everyone in the party experienced a meeting with some of the Ancestors, even the most skeptical among the crowd, although most present were there because they had had many such experiences in their lives. We visited an ancient Ancestor kauri tree, over one thousand years old we were told, whose base had been carved out by fire or time, leaving enough space inside it to hold 12 children or eight adults comfortably. This tree was a great communicator and all had beautiful insights and impressions in there.

As the Maori people walk into their forests, approaching such an Ancestor, they call out to their old people all the way. They sing a *waiata* of greeting, much as those of us in Australia who walk the land in this deeply connected way pause and silently or aloud state our business, that we come with love and respect and ask permission to enter, taking us into a deeper dimension of contact with the earth's spirit. This forest is filled with birds that respond to the presence of the people who are aware that they are entering the birds' home and territory.

The Maori women demonstrated their form of massage or *mirimiri* while others exchanged their forms of healing. There was sharing, walks, music and general enjoyment. Most present, about 60 in all, had interesting spiritually connected backgrounds and experiences to share with each other.

CHAPTER 28

The Phoenix meets the Whale

I remained in Te Kuiti for two or three years, living and working with the Maori people. In this region I really entered into the tunnel of darkness and heaviness still felt in the Maori world. My spiritual journey was more intense than ever but experiences are too numerous to mention here and were beyond the main subject of this book, which is about breaking the barriers and bringing certain aspects into a state of union rather than separation. I was given one last river task with Rangi, which involved the Phoenix meeting the Whale. The Phoenix rose higher than even the Eagle and the Whale travelled deeper than even the Serpent, which meant that further dimensions were coming into a unified energy. When walking in the hills which surround Te Kuiti I would see the form of a Phoenix rise in the sky, followed by a whale's tail and I would see the same in flames rising from the wood fire we had at home.

One day I took two friends to a favourite concealed cave of mine and when inside the cave, which lead onto one of these long underground tunnels filled with water, I sang a song in Gaelic and listened to the sound as it reverberated through the underground tunnels. When the sounds faded, instead of the expected silence, we all heard a song being sung back to us. It was a favourite Tieke song about the birds eating berries. Some would eat sweet berries and have sweet talk and some eat sour berries and the talk becomes sour. One gets used to just accepting this kind of phenomena in Aotearoa and does not look for a logical explanation. The old Maori people interacted very strongly with the environment and left their imprint everywhere in nature.

The song to me was Tieke calling me to work with the aspect of the Phoenix meeting the Whale. In this case I was the instrument for the Phoenix energy and Rangi that of the Whale. I did not hold out much hope of Rangi participating physically in this although I always felt his spirit around when required and no longer worried about what was to become of him, as that was his choice. I only felt saddened for the loss his family and people would experience.

During the six long weeks I was working with this energy I constructed a beautiful large garden at Tieke and left it ready for vegetables to be planted. I worked on this garden every day to keep myself grounded, as I would otherwise have floated off somewhere never to be seen again. A garden was not really needed there and indeed the river rose shortly after that and swept it all away. The work was done and I returned home first to Te Kuiti and then to Australia.

Shortly after I arrived at Glastonbell I was told that a phone call had come for me from Wanganui. Rangi was in hospital critically ill and may not live. I immediately went to the meditation cabin and tuned into his spirit. I saw his ancestors all around his head and it felt to me like he was in great conflict and being asked to make a final choice. That choice was his and his alone, of course, and there are no rights or wrongs when it comes to choices, only different consequences. I still felt he was making the choice to leave.

Sometime later I found myself eating some mulberries from a laden tree outside the house and thinking of the Tieke song, which Rangi among others used to sing. It was the song I had heard coming out from the cave at Te Kuiti. The berries were ripe and sweet and I felt as if his spirit had left the earth plain and was flying freely. As I approached the main house, a friend appeared in the doorway to say Rangi has gone. He was in his early forties and left behind a young family so it took me a little while to reconcile my part in his life and death. As I walked up the long driveway to collect my mail there seemed to be hundreds of birds flying all around me and the connection in spirit was still there. The following day I left for Sydney. I had arranged to visit a Maori healer, who had also known Rangi and would also have heard the news. I spent the first night in Sydney with another friend who asked if I would like her to give me a Reiki healing. As she was placing Reiki symbols on my back, Rangi's spirit came in and he said he wanted to draw his symbols on my back. Then he drew two simple symbols:

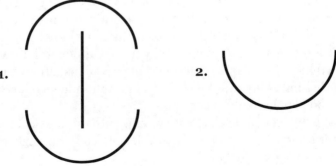

The next day, as I was walking to the house of my Maori friend, Rangi explained the first symbol to me with the words, "End of polarities. We now work as one." The second symbol represents water. This made sense to me and I felt quite relieved that all was indeed well. It was not long before I started to hear that all the other guardians of the river whom I had written my letter to asking permission to work with Rangi had also died, some within a few weeks of each other. There were about eight of them in all and some great old people left to make way for the younger ones to carry on with the next phase of the work.

CHAPTER 29
Umutja – First Attempt

The next stage of my journey took me to Alice Springs in Australia. I was to rent a house for a year and needed to have access to a Toyota Landcruiser. It was NAIDOC (National Aboriginal and Islander Day of Conciliation) week and I drove a Maori friend to a concert where he was performing at Telegraph Station. There I was introduced to a friend of his who asked me if I would like to rent his place for a year while he was away. The rent was reasonable and it was fully furnished. The date it was to become available was the day I had to leave my present accommodation. A few weeks after installing myself in this place, a friend arrived from overseas to join me. She provided the Landcruiser.

For someone who lives without financial resources this would be a tall order without the trust in the universe that comes with this way of living. I felt it was time to see Mantatjara again and visit a cave I could see with my inner vision and which was starting to call me to it. The cave was at Umutja and was the place where the grandmothers had walked, sat, danced and sung carrying the stone, which Mantatjara had given me to walk the land with.

Although the long, desert journey is generally tackled by Toyota these days, it was not like that when Mantatjara was growing up with her grandmothers. In those days it must have been a sheer delight walking or riding on camels or horseback with these old medicine women who knew the land so well and were so closely connected with their Ancestors, whose spirit still resides in the land. This would be the place where I would discover that my part in breaking the barriers between the Aboriginal and Celtic races had been accomplished and my intense work would come to an end.

With the help of my Pleiadian connections, I had been taken back to the time before entering into this body and had been shown the main tasks of my entire earth journey, its purpose, which was also my spiritual goal, and the results – if I were to commit myself to follow that goal to the end. Looking ahead I was allowed to see my chosen method of departure and time of leaving the earth to return to the spirit world and my next evolutionary journey, which would be in another realm where I have previously resided but which is also evolving.

Although it may seem far-fetched when in down-to-earth mode, my ancient memories were reawakened so that I recalled, as an instrument of the Creator, walking on this earth at the beginning of time, visiting these Sacred Sites, which seemed so familiar to me. Hence, in this lifetime it was truly like coming home when drawn there and I was given a glimpse of the Ancestral Beings from beyond the veil visiting earth to give to the Aboriginal people the initiation and increase ceremonies, the songs, songlines and stories.

This first attempt at reaching the destination of the cave at Umutja was aborted when clashes of personalities broke out around me. A spider bit me one morning as I woke up in my swag on the desert floor at one of the communities. We had been travelling for about ten days in the desert, including a sorry business stop, a football final and the harvesting of a crop of minkalbar (spelling guessed at), which is a native tobacco with a bit of a kick to it, and I was very hot and tired. There was no chance of being taken to these very sacred places if the energies were not right and I was accustomed to the fact that I had to be very quiet, very disciplined and have a still mind for that to happen. On this occasion my travelling companions were having arguments and it was becoming obvious to Mantatjara and I that it was not the right time to go to Umutja, so we abandoned the journey and I drove to the nearest clinic, which was at the tourist resort of Yulara, to see about the spider bite. By the time I arrived there the poison had entered my blood stream. Even so, I still hoped to heal the infection by natural methods when I returned home to Alice Springs. The nurse put a dressing on the festering hole which was appearing on my flesh and said I should get some antibiotics if it did not start to clear up in a day or two. At the motel I lay on the bed and started to drift in and out of consciousness and realised that my attacker had not been a benign little spider. It was in fact a pretty deadly Mulga spider.

I ended up at Alice Springs Hospital with antibiotics and daily dressings and swabs as ominous little outbreaks started to appear around the main one on my wrist. Spider bites can leave one almost paralytic and I stayed in bed hardly moving for several weeks. I may well have 'died' briefly as at the time a Maori friend in New Zealand had a dream whereby his deceased mother appeared telling him not to worry about Anne. I had crossed over but she had brought me back to finish my work. Realising something must have happened to me he contacted me to find out that I had in fact been weaving in and out of consciousness, bitten by a spider. Then the grandmothers came to me and asked me to remember the Maniopoto cave at Te Kuiti where I had seen Maya weaving the web of illusion and the spider weaving his web. The bite was a reminder to stay centred and detached on these spiritual journeys, no matter what was going on around me. It was vitally important not to get caught in a web of others' making, or in the spider's dance as Rangi had warned me previously at Pakaitore.

In Alice Springs I had plenty of time to contemplate my journey as I lay in bed recovering. I was being told that one more thing had to be accomplished before I went to the cave. This whole journey was about reconnecting, changing frequencies to bring energies into alignment with conditions for the new world and breaking the barriers. I was shown that I was to work with 'the ruby light of purification', followed by the 'golden light of recognition'. Then my purpose of breaking the barriers between the Celtic and Aboriginal race would be successfully completed and I could celebrate.

An interesting aspect of this sort of work is that there is no acknowledgement or accolades from earth people for what one has accomplished, which is why the timely appearance of rainbows, eagles and other gems from spirit are reassuring. By the same token before one is asked to take on anything like this one is put through many initiations and the ego is no longer jumping up and down requiring recognition. One has to keep a lot to oneself, which conserves the energy and preserves one's reputation as a reasonably sane human being.

The 'ruby light of purification' was being shown to me rising up out of a small cave. The 'golden light of recognition' rose out of a pool of water inside a larger, rounded, cave. The glow of the gem gave off enough light to see that there were several people seated around the pool, one of them being Mantatjara. The cave was right inside the rock known to millions from around the world as Uluru. To reach it I was to go along an underground passageway, at the same time following a timeline bringing together the Mayan, Hawaii'an, Maori and Celtic streams of consciousness from the past for recognition and purification. The 'Hawaii'an' was a new addition to my repertoire. I had absolutely no idea of where this passageway was or how to get there.

CHAPTER 30

The Ruby Light of Purification and the Golden Light of Recognition

As soon as I was mobile again I drove with a friend to the Mutitjulu community by Uluru, as I felt the time had come to work with the 'ruby light of purification' while my friend wanted to talk to some people she knew there. With a group of about seven Aboriginal women we were taken to a birthing cave at Uluru. We sat with the women in the cave and heard the story. They told us the story of how the first birth had been in that cave and that was a long time before the Aboriginal people came. I felt a stream of Ancestors come towards me and rush through me followed by a large black snake wearing a ruby coloured headband. We were then 'painted up' with symbols of the Seven Sisters, or Pleiades and joined in their ceremonies. Later, we were told that these women had been waiting for two white women to come and that evening as I was running down steps at our motel a pure white snake crossed my path, the sign from spirit that gave confirmation again. Although the snake was much whiter and very different from any seen in the area, I knew it was one which others could see, as a young boy had pointed it out excitedly to his mother. Later, I was to see a pure white cloud snake rise out from the top of Uluru, the background a deep blue sky, and turn around to face me before wriggling off – another confirmation.

Umutja – Second Attempt

When I next spoke to Mantatjara about going to Umutja, she said, "Do you want me to ask Nellie?" This was unusual because I always travelled with Mantatjara but I knew there must be a reason. I arranged with Nellie Paterson to meet her at Mutitjulu and we would drive to Umutja, this time by the shorter track to the north, about 250 kilometres from Kata Tjuta. I arrived at Mutitjulu one evening and she was waiting. She told me we would go with two of the elders the following morning. As usual the vehicle was loaded up with dogs, guns and digging sticks and with the old couple we set off for Umutja – or so I thought. We passed the Olgas, Kata Tjuta, and veered off to the left down the sand track which eventually leads to Umutja. About ten minutes later Nellie asked me to pull the vehicle over to the side of the track by the bushes. A fire was lit and the billy was put on the coals for a cup of tea. The old couple got out of the car and started digging for honey ants. I asked Nellie how much further it was to Umutja as I had no idea and she told me we were not going to Umutja and told me to go for a walk pointing towards the bushes. As I walked away from the group I felt the familiar trancelike state coming upon me and soon found my body lying on the ground in a catatonic state. I realised I was at the entrance of the passageway to the cave inside Uluru and made that journey to the 'Golden Light of Recognition'. I don't think it is wise to say too much more about that experience here as it happened very much in another dimensional reality. The importance of it was that it was a very necessary part of the journey of breaking the barriers which related to recognising each other as friends from a very distant past and that understanding bled through to the physical reality.

The old man who was with us was one of the traditional owners of Uluru and I felt strongly that it was he who had to oversee the journey. He died shortly after this and would be sorely missed by those he left behind. Nellie Paterson seemed to me to be his counterpart for the women's business. My business, of course, went beyond the men's and women's differentiation of business which was so important in their culture so on these occasions I noticed a male elder would be present with us.

When I was sharing this journey with a Maori elder he was most surprised that a non-Polynesian was allowed to make this journey into Uluru until he remembered that I had told him that I had Stewart blood on my mother's side of the family. Then to him it made sense because, he said, the House of Stewart goes back to the House of David and that made some sort of connection for him.

Chapter 31

The Cave at Umutja – Third Attempt

I was highly focused in one direction now, as I approached the end of my spiritual task, that of breaking the barriers between the Aboriginal and Celtic race, after which I liked to think I would be rewarded with an easy retirement. I had been rewarded many times in spiritual terms by being shown many sacred, secret places because of the courage I had shown but I had been all over the place in these last seven years on a shoestring and I was ready for the transition back to normal financial reality. I had been warned at the start of this indigenous journey that I would not have any money for a while and if I did have the tribal people would take it all from me, as part of my understanding of where they were coming from.

It was the year 2000. I drove down to Coober Pedy in South Australia, approximately 1000 kilometres south of Alice to the house where Mantatjara was staying. She had told me she had been painting and I had mumbled a casual response, as she was always painting. "No," she said, "I have been painting all week." Sure enough there was one of the most strikingly vital paintings I have ever seen leaning against the wall. It was of an enormous, powerful frilly neck lizard rising up into the cosmos.

We set off along the desert track to Pipalyatjara where she was to attend to sorry business due to the death of a close relative. As often happens on these desert roads we hit something not too far into the journey which flattened a tyre. As neither of us could work out the tools which had come with the vehicle and which in fact did not work, we had little alternative but to sit and wait until someone hopefully would turn up. The other alternative was to drive on the rim of the flattened wheel, which was the alternative Mantatjara chose. Thank goodness someone turned up before long and changed the tyre for us. We still had thousands of kilometres ahead of us with no spare or hope of getting one, so once again we were in the lap of the Gods, so to speak.

We did manage to reach Pipalyatjara eventually and one week was spent at the bush camp not far from the community where sorry business continued after the funeral service. As usual the energy of the place was making me feel heavy and nauseous. I found that around the communities one could be going around in circles getting nowhere, as if caught in the astral dramas of the past and present. This was part of my journey, of course, and it behoved me to observe from the sidelines or I would most definitely not reach my goal, in this case the cave at Umutja.

Eventually, after a few abortive attempts at getting the tyre fixed and ordering another in by plane from Kalgoorlie which ended up in Alice Springs, Mantatjara said we would travel on to Umutja, which until then I had always had in my mind as 'Omoju' as the name had come from spirit and I had never seen it written. Another grand old couple and their son were coming with us. Harry, following by at least ten of his dogs, was loading up the car with swags and guns as quickly as he was unloading the hounds. "No dogs," he said, but two managed to slip the net and off we went into the great beyond with no spare tyre, the window open ready to aim at kangaroos or whatever else might be good for dinner. Mantatjara was at the wheel. It was agreed that I was the bitumen driver and she the bush driver and she knew her land extremely well, driving through it was second nature to her. Luckily, because we were not on a track for much of the time, not one could see with the naked eye anyway.

The first night we camped out under a very clear starry sky with dingoes howling all around in a spinifex and wildflower valley surrounded by hills silhouetted in the light of the moon. The others slept around the campfire but I preferred to be at a distance from the smoke to enjoy a good night's sleep. I did not sleep much, however, as I wanted to savour the beauty and holiness of this night in this special place.

The following morning the old man indicated a cave high up on one of the hills near our camp. He told me its significance and asked me to walk up there and not be surprised if the hill seemed to change, sometimes high and sometimes low, as often happens in these very high vibrational places.

The old man (Billy Wara's brother) said I was a sister to him (Mantatjara translated for me) and that I could travel anywhere I wanted on Pitjantjatjara lands without a permit. This was probably because Mantatjara had been challenged by one of the white women in administration about bringing me onto the Aboriginal lands without a permit. In principal, I always regard the elders and traditional owners of the land the ultimate authority on that and not the bureaucrats, so I have never worried too much about permits.

When I returned from my walk the men had gone hunting and the two other women and I went to the women's sacred area. The entire area is mystical and magical and we passed many important sites on the way to the cave that I had felt such a strong desire to visit for over a year. We turned off the track to the right and straight in front of us I came face to face with the cave. Mantatjara said, "It's all yours." The two women drove off to harvest some medicine far beyond.

With tears streaming down my face I climbed over the rocks to enter the cave. I knew it well and without hesitation lay down on a raised rock inside the cave whose shape resembles that of an ancient Egyptian tomb. As I placed my head on the part shaped like a head, a sound emitted from my body that was unlike anything I had ever heard and one that I could not repeat in my normal state. The sound was deep at first and slowly rose to a very high pure note and I felt my body gradually disappear until only sound was left coming up from the rock and I was able to look down on it and watch. I was clearly reminded of having been here in earlier times to work with the frequency of this cave and here I was again back on earth in time for the next adjustment. This sort of experience happened many, many times during the years of working with the earth energies but somehow this one was the ultimate, being the end of a long but rewarding journey for me. After a timeless hour or so I came down from the cave feeling as light as a feather.

The Toyota and I arrived at the same point below together and as I was climbing into the front passenger seat Mantatjara said, "Look at the sky." It was the time solar flares were seen over the desert skies and we watched as slowly the whole sky became covered in delicate rainbow colours, then next to us appeared a very, very bright rainbow close to the ground, a few drops of rain fell and a large eagle had come to be with us, observing from a branch close by. We started the car up and drove off feeling that we must be doing something right! End of *mahi*. Time to retire! Instantly I heard the no-nonsense words, "Now you are to go to Scotland via Hawaii."

I realise that Mantatjara would not necessarily relate to my story if I shared some of my impressions with her but she just accepted what it was we were being guided to do without asking questions and our relationship survived because we gave each other that space of respect.

CHAPTER 32

Hawaii – The Frilly Neck Lizard

Mantatjara's painting of the Frilly Neck Lizard ascending to the heavens had made a strong impression on me. Just before leaving for Umutja I had bought a silk scarf with a large frilly neck lizard on it. I had dreamed my dog was standing at the door, pounding his front paws up and down on the concrete then turned his head to the left, again and again. I was laughing at him then got up to investigate. In the garden was an enormous frilly neck lizard. I wondered what this lizard wanted from me.

After Umutja, Mantatjara went to the Olympic Games in Sydney as one of the co-ordinators of the dancing ceremony, which was performed by the desert women. A friend who attended the Olympics said that a group there had tuned into archetypal serpent energy at Homebush Bay. Its message was that the reptilians were ready to let go of their controlling aspect but that there was trouble with the frilly neck lizard as it was angry and reluctant to move on, which explained to me the connection I was having with this creature. The reptilians wanted to release the controlling part of themselves through the lava tubes in Hawaii. By then I had bought my flight ticket to London via Honolulu with my credit card and had seen a round dark shape in my inner vision, which I took to be a cave.

Before I set off on my journey, I retreated to a quiet place in the country where nobody would find me. The telephone and electricity were disconnected and I only had candles and woodstove. My daughter dropped me off leaving me without transport. No one else knew I was there. I had little food but plenty of fresh clear water as I intended fasting and tuning into spirit to clarify the forthcoming journey. Just after midnight on about the third day of my stay, there came a knock at the door. It was a friend whom I had not seen for some years. She had just returned from Hawaii and knew she would find me here. We talked for a bit about our journeys and she gave me a medallion to hold and see what it said to me. First of all I received the picture of a gold coloured orb and crown, which was bent back at the top like a Tibetan headdress. Then I saw a conch shell and it told me the owner of the medallion had inherited a particular healing art to do with the conch shell and the ocean but which he was not using. My friend told me the regal part made sense as the medallion had been given to her by a Hawaii'an Arikinui or High Chief who was the equivalent of the king in Hawaii'an terms. For ceremonies he wore a golden crown just like the one I had seen in my vision. I found out about the conch shell later when I found one in his house. My friend said she had come because she thought I should meet this Hawaii'an friend and I knew I would need an indigenous Hawaii'an person to take me where I needed to go on the land, as usual. This has to do with the Ancestors opening the doors to other realms as much as anything and it only happens in the way I need it to happen if I go through the one who has been caring for the sacred site.

I wrote to this elderly Hawaii'an couple to say that we had a friend in common and that I was coming to Hawaii and they replied that they were waiting for me and would pick me up when I arrived at The Big Island of Hawaii where they lived at Kailua Bay. This couple kindly drove me all around the island to the Hawaii'an sacred places. I enjoyed some moving singing, dancing, drumming and above all chanting by the sea. We spent some time at the taro patch staying in their tiny house in the mountains surrounded by tropical flowers of every fragrance and colour, which they used to make their decorative lei. It was in a forest of tropical fruit trees, bananas, guavas of every description, mangoes, pawpaws, avocados, coffee beans and pineapples and they would go there regularly to look after the gardens and gather the fruit and taro. The taro grew in square patches in water, which flowed gently out of a cave at the top of the mountain and ran down the centre of the land in terraces. We picked coffee beans to sell. The couple took me everywhere in the hope of finding where I had to go and were worried in case they could not find the place, which I thought was a cave by its appearance in my vision. I did not worry at all about that as I knew from experience they would be guided to the right spot and I needed to have this gentle introduction to the land rather than barge into the place where I had to work.

Eventually they stopped, without making much of it, at a lava tube and let me go down to it alone. Suddenly, I felt an enormous rush of energy go through me and into the tube and I remembered the frilly neck lizard and the lava tube. I stayed in there for a while until I heard some worried voices calling for me. We drove up to a crater where the fiery, jealous Goddess Pele is said to reside in all her voluptuous magnificence. My hosts told me they perform ceremonies there with the people when they feel their culture is under threat by the Mainlanders – the U.S. Government.

The crater is still very much alive and smouldering and once again the uncontrollable tears started to stream down my face and I was left alone for a while. I sat by the crater until I felt the frilly neck lizard was at peace and released the controlling part of him up out of the crater and back to the stars. Such releasing of energies, whether reptilian, archetypal or of the earth, are not unlike a personal healing when there is someone supporting a friend or patient to release trauma.

As I left the house of my generous hosts I spotted a large conch shell amongst some books. I asked what it was for and was told it was used for healing in the old days. The Hawaii'an connection was coming into my journey with the Celts and Scotland, as both had been mentioned as part of the timeline in the cave at Uluru. The only indication I had received about my Scottish trip besides visiting relatives and friends was that I was to find the Stone of Destiny and activate it.

CHAPTER 33
Scotland and the Knights Templar

After a two and a half hour wait at Los Angeles Airport in the middle of the night we boarded the Lufthansa flight headed for London via Frankfurt. At Frankfurt I had the suspicion that the airport staff and I were not understanding each other about my luggage. That suspicion was correct and I arrived at Heathrow Airport in London at 9 p.m. without luggage and a message on the answering service of the friend I had hoped would pick me up to say he was unable to come. That meant I had to stay in a very comfortable, expensive hotel near the airport for the night and have my luggage couriered to a friend's place in Wiltshire where I would be staying the following night. It also meant that I slept for 15 hours straight instead of staying up all night with my friend and being exhausted.

The following morning I discovered that England had become a series of floating islands. The flooding was so bad that no one wanted to hire me a car, trains were at a standstill and coaches would only be travelling to certain places where the roads were still open. That cut out most of the friends I wanted to visit while in England. However, I did manage to catch a bus, then a train to Wiltshire where over three or four days my friend took me to Silbury Hill, Avesbury and in gum boots, we walked across the paddocks adjacent to my friend's house where crop circles are formed each year. We visited ancient Druid sacred areas and burial places. Unable to reach my friends in Cheshire, I telephoned my sister in Yorkshire who told me her daughter was now living with her family in Wales on the Cheshire border and the road was open to her place. I rang my niece and she met me from the train. We got the map out and my niece knew of some ancient sites we could visit. She had attended a Welsh university with Welsh-speaking students who were passionate about their history. However, two days later my sister turned up with a horse and horsebox and spirited me off to her home in Yorkshire. I had not seen my sister for about 14 years and after another two days was just settling in when my cousin from Scotland rang up to say he was working just south of where my sister lived and he would pick me up on his way through and drive me up to his home in St. Andrews, Scotland. Not a minute was being wasted and I was north of the border well before I intended.

The next day my cousin was driving to Edinburgh for some work he had to do there so he dropped me off at Roslyn Chapel, the old headquarters of the Knights Templar in Scotland and now a renowned Anglican church. It was, unfortunately, plagued by visitors drawn by its architectural and historic significance. I was not sure what to expect here but while in Wiltshire my friend had given me a book to read. It was the autobiography of Prince Michael of Albany who, descending from the Royal House of Stuart, is one of the claimants to the elusive Scottish throne. In this book he mentions the Stone of Destiny and its historic significance as well as Roslyn Chapel.

My cousin sped off to work leaving me at the entrance to the chapel, which proved closed to visitors that morning due to a wedding. After a cup of tea I wandered around the buildings and burial grounds and came upon a sign saying Freemasons, with an arrow pointing upstairs. Due to the fact that the place was closed I found myself alone up there midst all the regalia, photographs and all sorts of information about Freemasonry. I sat down and closed my eyes. In the old days those who headed the Knights Templar and Masonic Lodges were party to very advanced knowledge, which was used for the good of mankind initially but inevitably distortion crept into their systems. There was the Inquisition and many religious and political battles fought, leaving much to be brought into alignment. I felt a lot of energy of a purifying nature pass through me as I sat there and when I left I felt a lot lighter in body. The guests were now leaving the church and I looked at a few tombstones of Templars outside until the last had left. Again I had the chapel to myself and felt strong ancient energies pass through me as I sang a purifying song, which was provided by spirit for the occasion. There was nothing exceptional or unusual about any of this only that it was linking into the Celtic part of my story.

On another occasion my cousin dropped me off at Edinburgh Castle on his way to work so that I could have a look at the so-called Destiny Stone or Stone of Scone, which is now lodged in a glass case there. This stone is the one which has resided in Westminster Abbey since the 13th century when Henry IV Plantagenet subjugated the Scots and transported their regalia to the south of England. It has been placed under the throne whereupon the Monarchs of Great Britain have been crowned over the years. Many people, especially in Scotland, believe that the priest hid the true stone, probably at the time of the invasion and defeat and that a replacement was put in its place. They believe that the true Lai Phail, or Fatal Stone, is still hidden somewhere in Scotland and will one day re-emerge when the Scottish people regain their sovereignty. Various myths and mysteries have centred on what happened to the stone and where it may now be closeted safely away. When I saw the sandstone block in its glass case in Edinburgh Castle it bore no resemblance whatsoever to the one I had seen with my inner vision. It was devoid of energy and did not bear the symbols and markings I had seen. It was also the wrong colour, therefore the wrong stone and not the one I was to find. Nothing could activate this one.

Among the myths, legends and truths bandied about is one that confirms my messages from spirit declaring the stone of my inner vision was the stone mentioned in the *Bible* whereupon Jacob rested his head and heard God speak to him. This would make sense to me as the journey I am on takes me to places or objects, which are to be activated to realign with the pure energy, which flows through from universal mind of God. It is said that the prophet Jeremiah brought over this pillow to Ireland when he travelled from Egypt with Tara, the first Queen of Ireland, and later Dalriada, which combined Scotland and Ireland, and the stone came to what is now Scotland. The first King of Scotland, Scota, who also hailed from Egypt, was crowned standing on the stone. Various Monarchs followed, including the Stuarts, and each had to stand on the stone, recite their genealogy back along the Messianic lineage and swear allegiance to the people of the land. The Stone is said to hold the Messianic code, which is why it was of such great significance to Scotland (and England).

The time has still not come for me to be magnetised to that stone, although I am intending to return to Scotland early next year. I have received emails from people in Scotland keeping me up to date with what is published in newspapers and magazines, like the *Scottish Banner*, saying that the stone was last seen at the property of an Angus McGoig Hamilton and may be hidden in the vaults of a castle on Hamilton lands. However, I will only find it by following the intuitive urge when the time is right and I have no doubt that a worthy indigenous Scot will be the one to open that door for me. I was greatly surprised when, on my return to Australia, I heard that I would be going to Israel later on in the year and that I would meet the Wiltshire friend who would be there with a group in November.

CHAPTER 34
Jerusalem - Israel

I received an email from WWV, Wholistic World Vision, informing me of my Wiltshire friend's itinerary and noted that he would indeed be in Israel with a group in November. I was still repaying my credit card for the airfare and expenses to Scotland the previous year so I placed the idea of Jerusalem on the back burner. In Sydney I was visiting a friend who had been ill and had not ventured out of the house for a while, so I suggested we take the ferry and cross the Sydney Harbour to the Rocks, which is close to where the ferry comes into port. I wanted to call on Ulli, a healer who works with sound and who owns a shop at the Rocks. We met and the following day she took me to a park close to where she lived, as she was interested to see what I would pick up about the energy of the place. As usual when I meet someone who is interested in earth energy work I was relating a few anecdotes when she asked me if I was going to Jerusalem for the Light Summit that was being convened by Michael Lightweaver, the founder of the Planetary Awakening Network (PAN). This was interwoven with the group Peter Fuller was bringing over from the UK. She offered to pay for my ticket and expenses, saying that she would appreciate my company and could easily afford it. I have learned to be careful of people offering money as they may well have a hidden agenda, so I said I would sit with it and it was quite a few weeks later that it came to me that I would be able to return the favour another way later on and that she would come to Umutja with me. The money would be given unconditionally. I emailed my friend to say that although I had little chance of repaying her financially I felt I would like to accept her offer. By this time she had given up the idea of going to Jerusalem as she would not have gone alone and she had not heard from me. We made a late booking, and then the Twin Towers went down on September 11th. My friend, panicked momentarily and rang me up to tell me that she, like many others, was cancelling but that she would love to pay for me to go.

Finally, we both arrived in Jerusalem and unpacked our bags at the Knights Palace Hotel in the old city where the Summit was to be held. We met Peter and the group travelling with him. By this time I had received guidance about the purpose of my visit. I was to work with a pool of water under a church, which a friend had suggested could be the Coptic Church, and visit the Church of St. Anne and reactivate the Bethesda pool. I was not sure whether this was one and the same thing as I had no concept of what Jerusalem was like. The first morning I rushed out of bed early along the old narrow streets trusting that I would be drawn to the pools quickly as there was not much time before our group would be leaving for a three-day retreat at Qumran with Victor, our Israeli guide, who worked with the earth energies in that area.

I went straight to the Church of St. Anne, had a quick look, said hello to the spirit guardians but left without seeing any pools of water and thought they had perhaps dried up over the years. Then I raced back up the narrow streets and collided with a young boy who was carrying a basket of rolls balanced with one hand above his head. Together we picked up the rolls and I asked him if he knew where the Coptic Church was. He said we were standing outside it and when I looked up I saw a priest with long back gown and black headdress standing in a doorway. I asked him if this was the Coptic Church and he confirmed it was, asking me if I wanted to go to the pool of water, as if he had been waiting there for me to arrive. I cannot imagine many people wanting to go to the pool of water rather than the church. We walked through the little church, across a courtyard, down a flight of stone steps, past a small alter where a priest was reading, and finally he pointed to a dark narrow passageway with muddy, slimy stone steps and left me to descend to the large pool of water in this dark cavern. I was told that I was to work with the crocodile energy down here. I stayed for a few minutes announcing my purpose then sped back to the hotel in time to have a quick breakfast and join the others in two cars to drive down to the Dead Sea and Qumran where we were accommodated in comfortable chalets at a Kibbutz.

Each morning we walked to the ruins of the Essenes ancient habitat and sat to welcome the sunrise over the hills of Jordan across the water. By day we bathed in the Dead Sea and mineral hot pools, enjoying mud baths at both and in the evenings we would meditate up in the caves at Qumran where the Dead Sea Scrolls had been found.

It was quite a climb up to the caves and there were 11 in our group. As the first cave was a smallish rounded one, I am wondering how we all managed to be inside there together. The first night in the cave I thought I was imagining things, then a heard a voice calling, "Ishmael! Ishmael!" After hearing it several times I realised that some disembodied energy was trying to contact us. Then I heard, "An ancient curse has been put upon this land. It is time for it to be lifted." I was then shown energetically the way it would be lifted. A flame was coming up from the earth, through my body and it went up to join the seven flames of the Jewish Menora, 'To the Seventh Heaven'. From there it blended into one flame and rose up through the Crescent of the Arab world, 'To the Thirteenth Heaven'. At the time of receiving this transmission I had no idea who Ishmael was and had less than scant knowledge of Menoras, Crescents, Seventh and Thirteenth Heavens, so I made enquiries with members of the group to increase my understanding of what was being asked of me.

The following morning, while watching the sunrise over Jordan, I sat with the flame expecting that it might arise with me and would purify the energy of the curse. It did but only as far as the seven flames of the Jewish Menora, as Michael chanted, "Kodoish, Kodoish, Kodoish, Adonai 'Tsebayoth," praising God and calling in the archangels. The vibration of the chant seemed to be influencing the flame. However, it stopped short at the Menora and would go no further. Believing that I needed more information I invoked the ancestors. They appeared before me as three Toth-like Beings, with whom I had contact many times previously in New Zealand. They declared that all was well but that the curse would not be completely lifted until the end of the Summit.

When we returned to Jerusalem for the Light Summit there was not a great deal of free time as we used the days together for maximum benefit. However, before it started I raced down early in the morning to the Church of St. Anne. I was clearly being asked to reactivate the water in the pools of Bethesda behind the Church of St. Anne. This time I arrived before the grounds of the Church were officially open so I slipped past the office area and managed to have a good look around. There were some steps, which lead down to a platform with a railing whereby one could look down on a body of water but could not have access into the water and I did not feel any energy working to reactivate it. Normally, one would at least have one's hands in the water if not actually entering into it. I turned to leave when a priest came running down and asked me if I wanted to go into the water. I said I did but could not get down. Then he showed me how to climb over the railing and with help he guided my foot to a small peg on the other side. I did what was necessary, sang a song and the priest then helped me out again and left. Once again I was alone in a place, which is normally teaming with tourists. I sat quietly connecting with the spirit of

The cave at Qumran, Israel.

St. Anne, the grandmother of Jesus, and was awarded with a few drops of rain confirming that the work was done. Later, a small group returned with me and each gave the water their blessing in their own way and with their individual gifts.

The summit attracted around 60 highly evolved individuals from around the world and was a very powerful gathering. We would sit in a large circle under a glass pyramid set in the roof of the conference hall at the Knights Palace Hotel where we stayed for the duration of our time in Jerusalem. Many individuals and groups from around the world supported our morning and evening daily meditations as they were unable to attend in person, including those discouraged by the events of September 11th.

After a settling in period we actively cleared the energy of the space invoking the higher realms to be present with us. The energy of the morning meditations reached very high levels and drew a large column of light down through the glass pyramid and into the core of the earth. The group continued to bring light down into the earth through the vortex created in the hall and by the last day of the Summit the frequency was high enough to lift the curse, as promised.

Again Michael was chanting, "Kodoish, Kodoish," and, melding into the sound, I found myself swimming with the giant crocodile in the huge water cistern underneath the Coptic Church, round and round in a dance – a trance dance. I felt once again the seven flames of the Menora ignite and rise up to the Seventh Heaven. At the same time Zahara of Egyptian/Iraqi descent had placed herself on the mat underneath the pyramid and inside the vortex. Her body was swaying and from the depth of her being her voice produced an Arabic chant of such power that at first it seemed to eclipse Michael's graceful rendering of Kodoish, as if in competition, which was necessary to raise the energy of the Light to its most powerful. Then the two sounds blended as one and at that moment I saw the crocodile was letting its blood and I continued to swim in the blood with him as the music pulsated around me, bringing the flame up through the Crescent to the Thirteenth Heaven. The energy in the room had reached an extremely high frequency for this to be able to happen.

Following the raising of the light energy, I felt an urgency to return to the crocodile in the water under the church, feeling great love and gratitude for this immense Being. A group of nine people accompanied me and some chose to come down to the water with me. With feet in the dark, dirty, muddy water I called him to me and felt myself vibrating in a gentle 'crocodile dance' motion, as many negative Beings left the earth plane to the accompaniment of the Aramaic Lord's prayer spoken into the echoing cavern by Peter and a beautiful sacred song from Bulgaria sung by Renia. He finally looked straight into my eyes, grinned broadly, turned around and swam off. I had been told to expect quite a backlash after releasing so much negativity so Zahara and others had stayed outside the church, holding hands to create a circle of light around the golden dome to help release some of these energies.

I had been almost addicted to watching Arab funerals on the hotel television in the early mornings because this call to the mosque was so powerful and was very similar if not identical to the sound from Zahara, which lifted the energy so high.

After the Summit and on our last day in Jerusalem, the 11th November, Isaac Holly, a paraplegic Israeli Summit delegate, who is very well read, told me that physical crocodiles once lived under what is now Jerusalem and were worshipped as sacred because they absorbed all the negative energies put into the land. I felt this crocodile in his watery dungeon was a very sacred Being and I felt the Ethiopian priests who guarded his demise were well aware of this.

The background history to this ancient curse eludes me but knowledge gleaned from local Israelis points to the sons of Abraham and his two wives. Hagar, the mother of Ishmael, was, according to some inter

Bethesda Pool, Church of St. Anne, Jerusalem.

pretations, the spiritual partner to Abraham. However, Abraham married Sarah and Israel was born. Israel became the male principal, Jewish, Jehovah, the Light, while Ishmael became the female principal, Arab, Bileil, the Hidden, the Dark. The lifting of this curse would unite the brothers and the two streams of consciousness as one, and let us hope that this unification will filter through into the physical one day.

CHAPTER 35
The Sacred Pool at Umutja

Umutja is a remote homeland of the Pitjantatjara people in the Northern Territory, the Red Centre and heartland of Australia. It is officially recorded 'T.B.E.' – meaning the settlement of this homeland is still to be established. The reason it is not yet established is its location in the desert, 250 kilometres southwest of Uluru and Kata Tjuta along a red sandy track, which gets washed out in places after heavy rains. It is too remote for the old people who hold all the stories, songs and dances for the ceremonies to live here without reliable and appropriate transport. In this case it means a Toyota Landcruiser, the best vehicle to reach the distant waterholes and other sacred areas which are not on visible tracks.

Several years ago the Australian government built three good houses at Umutja with flush toilets, laundry, showers and plenty of clean bore water for the traditional custodians, Mantatjara, Billy Wara and Nellie Paterson among others, so that they could care for their land. Abundant bush medicine and bush tucker, such as wild figs, bush tomatoes, etc., can be found in the area as well as local meat from wild animals such as kangaroo, emu and goanna, but attempts at living there by Mantatjara and Nellie have so far been unsuccessful in the long term due to the lack of appropriate transport and the consequent inaccessibility to daily and cultural needs. The challenge the old people and medicine people face with establishing this area is the isolation factor and they feel a great need to return at this time to look after this very special land.

Nellie Paterson told me there are as many as 50 sacred sites in the surrounding area with stories important for keeping the culture, and the earth herself, strong. The sites at Umutja hold all the strengths and stories of the Dreamtime Law for women from conception right through every period of their growth and life. When the women are able to hold ceremonies there at the appropriate times the spirit from the land strengthens them and keeps them healthy. To be denied this part of the culture weakens and confuses them. When returning from these places at Umutja one feels completely re-energised. Umutja is a place where spirit children wait and can be seen or sensed by all. In the old days the women would seek out these places when it was time for them to conceive a child

Women's cave, central Australia.

and connect with the spirit which was waiting to enter her womb and this is still practised today where possible. When I went to the caves with Mantatjara I could see in the distance tin roofs of the three houses shining in the sun and knew that I would be going there one day.

I began to see a very unusual pool of water set in a large rock at Umutja and as I was going to work with water on the Queensland coast, I decided to make my way across the top of Australia and down to Uluru to perhaps go to Umutja. The pool contained very potent healing water and when activated to align with the new energies would be a direct link to universal mind. I telephoned Mantatjara who asked me if I wanted her to ring Nellie. Once again this surprised me a little since I usually travelled with Mantatjara but I presumed that her jurisdiction, inherited from the grandmothers, was probably not in that area. I met a friend at Uluru and together we arranged to meet Nellie at Mutitjulu. We did spend time at the Rock and at Mutitjulu but the timing was not right to go to Umutja and I returned to the east coast to wait. I was told certain things had to take place before this activation.

After resting in the country for a while I returned to Alice Springs. The water was calling strongly to me and I arranged to go with Nellie to Umutja. However, flooding on the tracks bogged her vehicle and made the tracks impassable at that time. I was noticing how much of the water element had come into my work. The floods in England, the waters in Jerusalem, Cairns and now the floods and water hole in the centre of Australia. Water holds a very strong consciousness and is encoded with much wisdom.

A few months later I was asked to work with activating the golden grid. Many people have been involved with this activation in varying stages and now I was to rejoin this work. I returned to a cave previously visited with a friend. The name she gave for this cave was the 'White Snake Cave', due to a marking of a long snake in white ochre on the back wall. I was being told this part of the activation had to take place before the water at Umutja. On my first visit to this area my friend had asked me to lie in a tiny feminine cave, which had red ochre paintings on its wall. A very strong woman's voice came to me saying that it was time to align with the golden feminine expression over-lighting the Black Madonna, Quan Yin, Mother Mary and the many other goddess expressions that people had been contacting and working with. It was not within my experience to work with these expressions but I felt the golden aspect was important and perhaps the message was of more relevance to my friend who was very familiar with these expressions.

On this second visit, I picked my way through the scrub and entered the cave of the White Snake. After a short time in meditation with many impressions entering my consciousness, as these ancient caves are always encoded with a great deal of history, I found myself sitting up in a regal pose as I transformed into a giant golden eagle. As I surveyed the land before me a large white snake appeared raising its head towards mine, then over the top of it came an even larger golden snake and blended into the eagle. The Eagle meets the Serpent again and this time the snake had moved out of the white vibration and into the golden. When I looked at the white snake on the wall behind me I noticed for the first time that there were about a dozen eagle feet painted in golden ochre around it. Before I left I went briefly into the small women's cave and heard, "It is done." People who work with geomancy and spirit generally are always glad to hear these sweet words.

It was time to go to Umutja, so I rang Nellie who was living in one of the desert communities where it is a miracle to get hold of a person, and if one succeeds then one knows there is a good reason for it. I also contacted my friend in Sydney who had helped me get to Jerusalem as I felt very strongly that she was meant to come with me on this occasion. Nellie wanted both she and I to meet her where she was living, which meant a 200-kilometre drive down a sand track to reach her. We got the obligatory flat tyre about halfway down this track but luckily a carload of men from the community stopped and helped us out with great efficiency and humour. If anyone has seen the film 'Bush Mechanics' you will know what I mean! We had hired a spotless new Landcruiser from Hertz to make this trip, which was blood curdling at times. Nellie was waiting for us and she and Pannini, a medicine woman, hopped into the car with digging sticks, spades, a box of carved animals and swags (Nellie forgot the rifle) and we left for Mutitjulu, which was our first stop.

We spent the first night in our swags at the campground in Yulara because the desert women love Kentucky fried chicken and this was the last stop for a while where such delicacies could be found.

After doing business with the woman at the Mutitjulu craft centre, we finally made our way along the bitumen as far as Kata Tjuta and then headed off to the left. We were now on the track to Umutja with Nellie behind the wheel. These women are excellent drivers on the sand due to years of experience, no doubt, and knowing their land so well. We travelled through exquisite countryside, so peaceful and beyond the sounds and atmosphere of civilisation. We passed families of marauding camels and kangaroos, which broke Nellie's heart as she had forgotten her rifle and to her that was a good square meal. As a vegetarian I was so glad she had forgotten her rifle.

As we approached the area called Umutja, Nellie began to veer off the track and take us to sacred water holes and rock formations telling us ancient stories she received from a lineage of grandmothers, a very special treasure to inherit and one which is held dear to her heart. At one stage we were taken to a mound of rocks, which Nellie called 'The Doctor', because of the great properties it held for healing the spirit. As I closed my eyes and sang a soft song to the Beings there I became conscious of being surrounded by women and children in spirit. This was followed by some tall white Beings with tall rounded white headdresses who were dancing. It looked like a ceremonial dance and I wondered if it was these Beings who had given the *inma*, or dance, and story of this site to Nellie's grandmothers. Nellie and Pannini sat quietly under a tree and waited for us to finish our connection with this site then we got back in

131

the Toyota and drove off.

Not too far, however, because the front of the car was thoroughly wedged on the one and only large rock which was on the invisible track in front of us. There was no hope of anyone passing this way in the next month or so, never mind a mechanic or a tow truck, so perseverance reigned. I said to Ulli, my friend from Sydney, if it were just she and I who had found ourselves in this situation I would be starting to worry. However, I had great faith in these women getting us out of there. These people are very courageous and resilient and they do not give up easily, as to persevere is to survive in the outback. They jacked up the front of the car while we collected handfuls of grass and flat rocks to put under the wheels. They dug for two hours with their digging sticks until on about the third go of my reversing, while the others pushed, we finally broke free from the rock with just a slight ding and a few scratches under the otherwise perfect Toyota. A bit of boot polish and charcoal back home more or less fixed the damage.

That night we slept in our swags at Nellie's house. It was locked up and she had forgotten the key but that was unimportant, as we would have slept outside on the verandah anyway. We had a wonderful night of music and dancing together. Ulli, who works with sound healing had brought some musical instruments with her that the women enjoyed playing. Then we joined in *inma,* or women's dances, and Ulli recorded Nellie and Pannini singing. This was a song in the Pitjantjatjara language and was punctuated, and at times drowned out, with Nellie's coughing as she had severe chest problems on the trip and had almost lost her voice. That did not stop her making a determined effort to sing and hear her voice recorded on the tape recorder, which produced much laughter from all of us. The women always sing their songs as they approach a sacred site and Mantatjara has told me some are in a language much older than theirs.

As mentioned, Umutja is a place where spirit children live and they come to welcome any visitors. We all saw them in various forms. Umutja is a multidimensional place and one does not feel of this world in such places at the best of times. To cap this, nature gave us a spectacular treat with a full moon appearing and disappearing through dark cloud formations, followed by a terrific lightening display, which lasted intermittently with rolls of thunder all night long. We only had a few drops of rain meaning that we were not stranded there indefinitely. The sto

Nellie and Pannini gathering bush tomatoes on the road to Umutja.

ries when told on these sacred sites are very potent indeed and once again they are multidimensional so cannot be understood with the logical mind. They are energetic and historic and only reveal their full meaning in stages. They conceal the truth in myth. I have a long way to go before fully understanding some of them but many people who do not connect with the earth energies do not understand them at all.

There was one story in particular which really played on my mind and I did not fully understand it. Nellie and Pannini took us to a very large flat rock speckled with gold, which had a few small lumps in it at one end. From here the land went down a slight incline to a hole in the ground with water deep inside it. The earthy incline also was lumpy and the story was that this was the place where the babies were wrapped up and put into the earth. These were the lumps we saw and felt. Their blood went down and mingled with the water, which came up out of the waterhole as spirit. The children later got up but were weak and had to be helped. There was also a woman squatting on the rock breast-feeding two babies. A man walked past her and asked if she needed help and she told him to go away. A more general story of the place is that when they went hunting the men wanted to leave the children behind at home but the women said, "They have to come with us, we cannot leave our children." The energy around this place and story was so overpowering that I had the feeling I would need to return there one day to process and integrate it into my being. I did manage to capture the feeling of the Aboriginal spirit children who wait at these sacred places to enter a woman who wishes to conceive. I felt like it was a place where humans had been seeded by Beings from other realms back in the Dreamtime and where the spirits of future children await rebirth. Hopefully, such wisdom shall not be lost to humanity and rampant materialism due to the old people being unable to fulfil their important role, which is indispensable for the health and well-being of their people and our shared earth.

On the last night at Umutja it seemed to me that although I had had very strong experiences at the different waterholes we had stopped at, I still had not been to the one I could see in my vision. This one had water in a rock like the others but the water was in a pool above the ground, whereas the others were down in the ground like a well. We were leaving the following morning so I asked Nellie if there was another waterhole with water above the ground. She pointed towards the men's area and said we were going to that one tomorrow on the way home. Once there, I knew immediately from the feeling that came to me this was the pool I had envisaged. We drove to the area and my friend and I went over to the pool while the others waited patiently as usual. The pool had camel dung and grasses floating in it and did not look very pure but the energy testified to the saying that you cannot tell a book by its cover. I lay there and allowed the new frequency to filter through my body and into the rock, which held the water. After some time the energy faded and I sang a song while taking the water in my hands and putting a few drops on me to feel a physical connection with it. Then we got back into the vehicle. I wondered what these Pitjantjatjara medicine and senior law women thought about a white person's ways with this land to which they are so close. I have the impression they just accept it without thinking too much at all, which is a great blessing. The knowing eliminates the thinking.

CHAPTER 36

The Free Spirit

These are stories of a Free Spirit. Although psychic phenomena feature prominently in the weave of my stories, as a free spirit I have never felt the urge to follow any doctrine, group or belief system, nor have I felt the necessity. The words received by me come from a spiritual lineage; aspects of myself flowing down from Universal Mind and through my Higher Self, for want of a better expression. My Higher Self is my immortal spirit who, like the Eagle, has the overview of where my spirit needs to travel, whether on earth or elsewhere, for its evolutionary journey through space and time.

Because of certain unusual and difficult aspects of my situation and work, I was shown that overview of my entire life before conception and to the end so that I could see the weave before courage failed me. It is a beautiful weave of unification all the way to 'Omega Point' in the year 2012, when all who wish will have been given the greatest opportunities to understand and live the full meaning of 'heaven on earth'. I have chosen to live for a further four years to 2016 to enjoy the fruits before departing to other realms for my next journey. I have been shown the method I will use for departing which thankfully does not include hospital. Nor was it ascending in a spaceship or other means. When the time comes I will walk to one of my favourite places on the land, will sit down in deep meditation and drift off consciously forever, which has a certain appeal.

The barrier between the Aboriginal and Celtic races has been broken at the deepest of levels and we await the unfolding of the next phase of the grand vision when we truly have remembrance of why we are here. Nellie and Mantatjara have recently announced a very important sacred ceremony is to be held at Umutja next year with women, both Aboriginal and non-Aboriginal coming from all over Australia.

ENDS